THE
IRISH REBELLION *of* 1916
OR
THE UNBROKEN TRADITION

BY
NORA CONNOLLY

BONI AND LIVERIGHT
NEW   YORK

Copyright, 1918,
Copyright, 1919,
By Boni & Liveright, Inc.

Printed in the United States of America

LIST OF ILLUSTRATIONS

James Connolly		*Frontispiece*
Countess Markievietz	Facing page	12
Thomas J. Clarke	" "	36
The Proclamation of the Provisional Government issued at the G. P. O. on Monday, April 24, 1917	Facing page	44
John McDermott	" "	66
Nora Connolly	" "	88
Liberty Hall	" "	100
Joseph Plunkett	" "	118
Thomas Macdonagh	" "	134
Eoin MacNeill	" "	152
Patrick H. Pearse	" "	170
Eamonn Ceannt	" "	182

MAPS

	PAGE
The Journey from Belfast to Leek	22
The Journey from Dundalk to Dublin	23
Map of Dublin	Facing page 164

INTRODUCTION

THERE have been many attempts to explain the revolution which took place in Ireland during Easter Week, 1916. And all of them give different reasons. Some have it that it was caused by the resentment that grew out of the Dublin Strike of 1912-13; others, that it was the threatened Ulster rebellion, and there are many other equally wrong explanations. All these writers ignore the main fact that the Revolution was caused by the English occupation of Ireland.

So many people not conversant with Irish affairs ask: Why a revolution? Why was it necessary to appeal to arms? Why was it necessary to risk death and imprisonment for the self-government of Ireland? They say that there was already in existence an Act for the Self-government of Ireland, that it had been passed through the English House of Commons, and that if we had waited till the end of the war we would have been given an opportunity to govern ourselves. That they are not conversant with Irish affairs must be their excuse for thinking in that manner of our struggle for freedom.

To be able to think and to speak thus one must first recognize the right of the English to govern Ireland, for only by so doing can we logically accept any measure of self-government from England.

And we cannot do so, for, as a nation Ireland has never recognized England as her conqueror, but as her antagonist, as an enemy that must be fought. And this attitude has succeeded in keeping the soul of Ireland alive and free.

For the conquest of a nation is never complete till its soul submits, and the submission of the soul of a nation to the conqueror makes its slavery and subjection more sure. But the soul of Ireland has never submitted. And sometimes when the struggle seemed hopeless, and sacrifice useless, and there was thought to make truce with the foe, the voice of the soul of Ireland spoke and urged the nation once more to resist. And the voice of the soul of Ireland has the clangor of battle.

There have been many attempts to drown the voice of the soul of Ireland ever since the

INTRODUCTION

coming of the English into our country. There have been some who have had the God-given gift of leadership, but still sought to misinterpret the sound of the voice; who in shutting their ears to the call for battle have helped to fasten the shackles of slavery more securely on their country.

There was Daniel O'Connell who possessed the divine gift of leadership and oratory, and in whose tones the people recognized the voice of Ireland and flocked around him. During the agitation for the Repeal of the union between Ireland and England the people followed O'Connell and waited for him to give the word. Never for one moment did they believe that the movement was merely a constitutional one. Sensibly enough they knew that speeches, meetings and cheers would never win for them the freedom of their country. They knew that force alone would compel England to forego her hold upon any of her possessions.

So that when in 1844 O'Connell sent out the call bidding all the people of Ireland to muster at Clontarf, outside Dublin, they believed that the day had come, and from North, South, East and West they started on the journey. Those who lived in the West and South traveled the distance in all sorts of conveyances, many of them, especially the poorer ones, walked the distance; but the trouble, the weariness, the hardship were all ignored by them in the knowledge that they were once more mustering to do battle for the freedom of their country.

But in the meantime, while the people were making all speed to obey the summons of O'Connell, the meeting had been proclaimed by the British Government; and the place of muster was lined with regiments of soldiers with artillery with orders to mow down the people if they attempted to approach the meeting place. Then it was that O'Connell failed the people of Ireland, and rung the knell for the belief of the Irish people in constitutionalism. He said, "All the freedom in the world is not worth one drop of human blood," and commanded the people to obey the order of the British Government and to return to their homes.

There are many pitiful, heart-breaking stories told of the manner in which this command of O'Connell reached the people. Many who had walked miles upon miles reached the outskirts of Dublin only to meet the people pour-

INTRODUCTION

ing out of it. When in return to their questions they were told that it was the request of O'Connell that they return to their homes, the heart within them broke for they knew that their idol had failed them, and their hopes of freeing Ireland were shattered.

Within the Repeal Association there was another organization called the Young Irelanders, which published a paper called *The Nation*. This paper was an immense factor in arousing and keeping alive a firm nationalist opinion in Ireland. The Young Irelanders were revolutionists, and by their writings counseled the people to adopt military uniforms, to study military tactics, to march to and from the meetings in military order. They made no secret of their belief that the freedom of Ireland must be won by force of arms.

During the famine in 1847, when the people were dying by the hundreds, although there was enough food to feed them, the Young Irelanders worked untiringly to save the people. At that time potatoes were the staple food of the people, everything else they raised, corn, pigs, cattle, etc., had to be sold to pay the terrible rackrents. The Young Irelanders called upon the people to keep the food in the country and save themselves; but day by day more food was shipped from the starving country to England; there to be turned into money to pay the grasping landlords. It was during this time that John Mitchell was arrested and transported for life to Van Diemen's land.

In 1848 there was an ill-fated attempt at insurrection. Even in the midst of famine and death, with the people dying daily by the roadside, there was still the belief that only by an appeal to force and arms could anything be wrung from England. In Tipperary, under Smith O'Brien, the attempt was made, more as a protest then, for famine, death, and misery had thinned the ranks, than with any hopes of winning anything. Most of the leaders were soon arrested and four of them were sentenced to be hanged, drawn, and quartered; but this sentence was afterwards commuted to life imprisonment.

For many years after the famine the people were quiescent, and had grown quite uncaring about Parliamentary representation. And then was formed a revolutionary secret society calling itself the Fenians. The members of this organization were pledged to work for, and, when the time came, to fight for and establish, an Irish Republic. James Stephens was the chief organizer. The organization spread through Ireland like wildfire. Even the English Army and Navy were honeycombed with it. Every means possible were taken by the English to cope with this new revolutionary movement—but they failed. The organization decided that a Rising would take place in February, 1867. This was later postponed; but unfortunately the word did not reach the South in time and Kerry rose. The word spread over Ireland that Kerry was up in arms. Measures were taken by the English to meet the insurrectionists, but before they reached the South the men had learned that the date of the rising had been postponed and had returned to their homes. Luby, O'Leary, Kickham, and O'Donovan Rossa were arrested. Still the Rising took place on the appointed date, although doomed to failure owing to the crippling of the organization by the arrest of its leaders, and the lack of arms. Even the elements were against the revolutionists, for a snowstorm, heavier than any of the oldest could remember having seen, fell and covered the country in great drifts.

They failed. But the teaching of the Fenians and the organization they founded are alive to-day. It was the members of this organization that first started the Irish Volunteers. Ever on the watch for a ripe moment to come out and work openly, ever longing for the day when military instruction could be given to the nationalist youth, they seized upon the fact that if the Ulster Volunteers were permitted to drill and arm themselves to fight the English Government so could they. And in November, 1913, they called a meeting in the Rotunda, Dublin, and invited the men and women of Ireland to join the Irish Volunteers, and pledge themselves "to maintain and secure the rights and liberties common to all the people of Ireland."

So once more the people of Ireland heard the call to arms, and right royally they answered it. The Irish Volunteer Organization spread throughout the land, and the youth of Ireland were being trained in the art of soldiering.

Then it was that, like Daniel O'Connell and other constitutional leaders, Redmond proved himself of the body and not the soul of Ireland. He did not follow the example of Parnell, whose follower he was supposed to be, and use the threat of this large physical force party to

INTRODUCTION xv

gain his ends from the English Government. Parnell used to say to the British House of Commons: "If you do not listen to me, there is a large band of physical force men, with whom I have no influence, and upon whom I have no control, and *they* will compel you to listen to them." But Redmond, jealous of all parties outside his own (knowing well that when an Irishman had a rifle in his hands he no longer felt subservient to, or feared England; and that when the people of Ireland had the means to demand the freedom of their country they grew impatient of speech-making and petitioning), grew fearful for the loss of power of the Irish Parliamentary Party.

He knew also, that, as in the days of O'Connell, Butt, and Parnell, the people firmly believed that all the talk and show of constitutionalism was a blind, merely a throwing of dust in the eyes of the English Government, and to save himself and his Party he must approve this physical Force party. But not content with approval he needs must try to capture the Irish Volunteers. This attempt, I firmly believe, was made upon the advice, or the command of the British Government. He sent a demand to the Executive Committee that a number of his appointees be received upon the Committee. This would enable him to know and obstruct all measures made by the Irish Volunteers and would prevent the loss of power of the Parliamentary Party.

By the votes of a small majority of the Committee these appointees were accepted. But the Committee soon found out that it was impossible to arm and prepare men for a revolution against a government, while the paid servants of that government were amongst them. They decided to part company even at the risk of a division in the ranks. They knew that every man who remained with them could be depended upon to do his part when the time for the Rising came.

Then England went to war. Shortly before this a Home Rule Bill had passed two readings in the House of Commons. England saw the stupidity of appealing to Irishmen to go to fight for the freedom of small nationalities, while any measure of freedom was denied to their own. So the Home Rule Bill passed the final reading in the House of Commons, and was put upon the Statute Book. Then fearful of the dissatisfaction of the Unionists an amendment was tacked on that prevented its going into effect until after the war.

John Redmond dealt the final blow to his influence upon Ireland when he began to recruit for the English Army. Many of his followers, taking his word that Home Rule was now a fact entered the English Army at his request. They were, in the main, young, foolish, and ignorant fellows unable to analyze the Bill for themselves, and therefore could not know that the so-called Home Rule was a farce. They did not know that the Bill gave them no power over the revenue, over the Post Office, over the Royal Irish Constabulary, that they could not raise an army, or impose a tax, and that no law passed by the Irish Parliament could go into effect until the English House of Commons had given its approval. It was like telling a prisoner that he was free and keeping him in durance.

And from the beginning of the war the Irish Volunteers spent all the time they could in intensive drilling, not knowing at what time their hand might be forced, or the opportune moment for the Rising might arrive.

For in Ireland we have the unbroken tradition of struggle for our freedom. Every gen-

xviii   INTRODUCTION

eration has seen blood spilt, and sacrifice cheerfully made that the tradition might live.

Our songs call us to battle, or mourn the lost struggle; our stories are of glorious victory and glorious defeat. And it is through them the tradition has been handed down till an Irish man or woman has no greater dream of glory than that of dying

"A Soldier's death so Ireland's free."

THE IRISH REBELLION OF 1916
OR
THE UNBROKEN TRADITION

I

My first mingling with an actively, openly drilling revolutionary body took place during the Dublin strike of 1912-1913. I was living in Belfast then and had come to Dublin to see how things were managed, how the food was being distributed and the kitchens run; and, in fact, to feel the spirit of the people.

James Connolly, my father, was at that time in Dublin assisting James Larkin to direct the strike. He was my pilot. Liberty Hall, the headquarters of the Irish Transport and General Workers Union, the members of which were on strike, was first visited. It is situated on Beresford Place facing the Custom House and the River Liffey. In the early part of the nineteenth century it had been a Chop House. Almost from the big front door a wide staircase starts. It ends at the second story. From there it branches out into innumerable corridors thickly studded with doors. It took me a long time to master those corridors. Always I seemed to be finding new ones. Downstairs on the first floor were the theater and billiard rooms; and below them were the kitchens. During the strike these kitchens were used to prepare food for the strikers. It was to the kitchens my father first piloted me.

Here the Countess de Markievicz reigned supreme—all meals were prepared under her direction. There were big tubs on the floor; around each were about half a dozen girls peeling potatoes and other vegetables. There were more girls at tables cutting up meat. The Countess kept up a steady march around the boilers as she supervised the cooking. She took me to another kitchen where more delicate food was being prepared for nursing and expectant mothers.

"We used to give the food out at first," she said. "But in almost every case we found that it had been divided amongst the family. Now we have the women come here to eat. We are sure then that they are getting something sufficiently nourishing to keep up their strength." She showed me a hall with a long table in the center and chairs around it. As it was near the "Mothers' dinner hour," as the girls called it, some of the striking women and girls were there to act as waitresses.

We came to the clothing shop next. Some persons had caught the idea of sending warm clothing for the wives and children of the strikers; accordingly one of the rooms of Liberty Hall was turned into an alteration room. Several women and girls were working from morning to night altering the clothes to fit the applicants. One of the girls said to me, "It was a wonder to us at first the number of strikers who had extra large families, until we found out that in many cases their wives had adopted a youngster or two for the day, and brought them along to get clothed." Not strictly honest, perhaps, but how human to wish to share their little bit of good fortune with those not so fortunate as themselves. How many little boys and girls knew for the first time in their lives the feel of warm stockings and shoes, and how many little girls had the delicious thrill of getting a new dress fitted on.

Thence to Croyden Park. Some time before the strike this immensely big place had been taken over by the Union. I do not know how large it was but there were fields and fields, and long pathways edged with trees. It was used by the members as a football ground and for hurley and all sorts of sports and games. But this time the fields were ringed round with men and women watching the rows and rows of strikers who were in the fields, marching now to the right, now to the left at the commands of Captain White, who stood in the center, a tall soldierly figure blowing a whistle and gesticulating with great fervor.

Back and forth, right and left they marched with never a moment's rest; then round and round the fields they ran at the double; the Captain now at the head, now at the rear, now in the center shouting commands incessantly, sparing himself no more than the men. I remember once he stopped beside my father and myself; he was in a terrible rage, his hands were clenched and he was fairly gnashing his teeth. He had given a signal to one of the columns and they had misinterpreted it.

"Easy now, Captain," said my father, "remember they are only volunteers." Captain White turned like a flash.

"Yes," he said. "And aren't they great?"

And he forgot his rage in his admiration of the men of a few weeks' training. He gave an order, the men marched past and at a given place they received broom handles with which they practiced rifle drill.

After rifle drill came the line up for the march home. We waited till the last row was filing past and then fell in and marched back to the city with the Irish Citizen Army. It was exhilarating. At no period could I see the first part of the Army. The men and boys were whistling tunes to serve them in lieu of bands. On they swung to Beresford Place, where they lined up in front of Liberty Hall. Jim Larkin and my father spoke to them from the windows. When one man called out, "We'll stick by you to the end," he was loudly and heartily cheered. Captain White gave the order of dismissal and the men broke ranks but did not go away. When they were not drilling, or sleeping, or eating, they thronged round Liberty Hall, attesting that "where the heart lieth there turneth the feet."

When the strike was over and the men had won the right to organize, the membership of the Irish Citizen Army dwindled rapidly. When one takes into consideration the arduous work and the long hours that comprised the daily round of these men, the wonder was that there were so many of them willing to meet after working hours to be drilled into perfect soldiers. But they knew that by so doing they were, in the words of my father, "signifying their adhesion to the principle that the freedom of a people must in the last analysis rest in the hands of that people—that there is no outside force capable of enforcing slavery upon a people really resolved to be free, and valuing freedom more than life." Also that "The Irish Citizen Army in its constitution pledges its members to fight for a Republican Freedom in Ireland. Its members are, therefore, of the number who believe that at the call of duty they may have to lay down their lives for Ireland, and have so trained themselves that at the worst the laying down of their lives shall constitute the starting point of another glorious tradition—a tradition that will keep alive the soul of the nation." And this was the knowledge that lightened all the labor of drilling and soldiering.

I was present at a lecture given to them by their Commandant, James Connolly. It was on the art of street fighting. I remember the close attention every man paid to the lecture and the interest they displayed in the diagrams drawn on the board the better to explain his meaning. At the close of the lecture he asked, "Are there any questions?" There were many questions, all of them to the effect, whether it would not be better to do it this way, or could we not get better results that way. All in deadly earnestness, thinking only on how the best results might be achieved and not one man commenting on the danger to life the acts would surely entail. That one would have to risk death was taken for granted. Their one thought was how to get the most work done before death came.

A few months later there were maneuvers between one company of the Irish Citizen Army and a company of the Irish Volunteers. The Irish Volunteers had been formed after the Irish Citizen Army and by this time had spread over the length and breadth of Ireland. While the Irish Citizen Army admitted none but union men the Irish Volunteers made no such distinction. And as they both had the one ideal of a Republican Ireland there was much friendly rivalry between the two bodies. This time the maneuvers took the form of a sham battle, which took place at Ticknock about six miles outside of Dublin. The Irish Citizen Army won the day. I particularly remember that afternoon. My father came into the house, tired but pleasantly excited—he had been an onlooker at the sham battle. "I've discovered a great military man," he said in high glee. "The way he handled his men positively amounted to genius. Do you know him —his name is Mallin?"

I did not know him then. I met him later when he was my father's Chief of Staff. During the rising he was Commandant in charge of the St. Stephen's Green Division of the Army of the Irish Republic, and he was executed during that dreadful time following the surrender of the Irish Republican Army.

II

DURING the month of July, 1914, I was camping out on the Dublin mountains. The annual convention of Na Fianna Eireann (Irish National Boy Scouts) had just been held, and I was a delegate to it from the Belfast Girls' Branch, of which I was the president. On the Sunday following the convention we were still camping out; but were suffering all the discomforts of blowy, rainy, stormy weather. Madame (the Countess de Markievicz) had a cottage beside the field where we were encamped, and it was thronged with us all that Sunday. Nothing would tempt us out in the field that night, and we kept putting off the retiring time, hour by hour, till it was nearly twelve o'clock. At that time we had just taken our courage in both hands, and were forcing ourselves to go out to our tents. We were standing near the door with our bedding in our arms when some of the Fianna boys halloed from outside. We gladly opened the door—another excuse for putting off the evil moment—and about half a dozen boys came in to the cottage. They were in great spirits, although they had tramped some miles in the rain, and exhibited strange looking clubs to our curious eyes.

"Guess what we've been doing to-day, Madame," they said, but with an expression on their faces which said, "you'll never guess."

"It's too much trouble to guess," said Madame. "Tell us what it was and we will know all the quicker."

"We've been helping to run in three thousand rifles."

"Rifles—where—quick—tell me all about it. Quick."

"At Howth. But did you hear nothing about it?"

"Nothing. Tell me quick."

"Did you not hear that we had a brush with the soldiers; and that some were shot and some were killed?"

"No—no. Begin at the beginning and tell us the whole story."

"Well, during the week we were told to report at a certain place to-day—that there was important work to be done. This morning we met as we were told, and we were shown these clubs. They were to be all the arms we were to have. We started out to march with the Volunteers to Howth. We knew, somehow or other, that we were going to get rifles but none of us knew for a fact how we were going to get them. As we marched we made all sorts of guesses as to how the rifles were coming. Of course, we did not carry the clubs in our hands; we brought them with us in the trek cart. But for a few others we were the only ones who knew what was in the cart. And do you know, Madame," he said with a veteran's pride, "we marched better than the Volunteers."

"When we came near Howth," said another boy as he took up the story, "two chaps came running towards us and told us to come on at the double. The Volunteers were rather tired but when they heard the word 'rifles' they simply raced. When we arrived at the harbor we saw the rifles being unloaded from a yacht. You ought to have heard the cheers when we saw them! Then it was that the clubs were distributed. They were given to a picked body of men and they were formed across the entrance to the pier. They were to use the clubs

12 THE UNBROKEN TRADITION

if the police attempted to interfere with them. The rifles were handed out to the men, but there were more rifles than men so some had to be sent into the city in automobiles. Most of the ammunition was sent into the city in automobiles but quite a lot was put into the trek cart. But none was served out to the men."

"That was a nice thing to do," said the first boy, "to give rifles and no ammunition. And when we were attacked we couldn't shoot back. We had a fight with the soldiers and the police near the city. And when the soldiers and the police attacked us and might have taken the trek cart from us, we had only the butts of our rifles to defend it with. But we beat them off. Later on, though, they took their revenge when they shot down defenseless women and children. They just knelt down in the middle of Bachelor's Walk and fired into the crowd. I don't know how many were killed—some say five, some say more."

"But you brought the rifles safe," said Madame.

"The whole city is excited. The people are walking up and down the streets, they don't seem to think that they have any homes to go to."

When we heard that we wanted to dress and go down to Dublin. We wanted a share of the excitement, if we had not had any share in the fight. But Madame vetoed that suggestion almost as soon as it was mooted. We had to go to bed. But we had so much to talk about that we scarcely noticed the sogging wet tent when we were inside.

The next morning was gloriously fine. We breakfasted and were making plans to go into the city to hear some more about yesterday's exploit. Madame had already cycled in, and we were left to our own devices. We had not quite finished our work around the camp when we saw a taxi-cab stopping near the gate that was used as an entrance to the field. As we ran towards it we wondered what had brought it there. Before we reached it, however, one of the Fianna captains had jumped out of the taxi and was coming towards us.

"I have about twenty rifles in the car, and I want to get them to Madame's cottage," he said. "Will you help?"

We were glad of the opportunity. We jumped over the hedge into the next field where there were no houses, and had the rifles handed to us. We could only carry two at a time. The captain stood at the car on the lookout, and also handed the rifles to us. We carried the rifles down to the window back of Madame's cottage, and when we had them all there one of us went inside to open the window to take the rifles from the other girls as they handed them through. We were delighted to handle the arms.

Later on one of the neighbors said that it was wrong to leave the rifles there. "There is a retired sergeant of the police who lives a little way up the road and he wouldn't be above telling about them."

This rather frightened us. If the police came and took them from us, what could we do? I decided to go in to Dublin and go to the Volunteer office and tell them about the rifles. When I had told about the rifles two of the men present accompanied me back to the camp to take the rifles from there.

We set off in another taxi and arrived at the camp before there was any sign of the police becoming active. All the rifles were carried out again and put in the taxi. When they were all in it, it was suggested that we should get into the taxi and sit on top of the rifles. The police would be less suspicious of a taxi

THE UNBROKEN TRADITION 15

with girls in it. It was not a very comfortable seat that we had on that trip to Dublin. But the rifles were saved. When we got back to the office I offered to sit in any taxi with the rifles if they thought it would divert attention. I sat on quite a number of rifles that day. And at the end of the day I had a rifle of my own.

In the meantime, the bodies of those who had been shot by the soldiers were laid out and brought to the Cathedral. Preparations were made for a public funeral to honor the victims of English soldiery in Ireland. All the Volunteers were to march in honor of the dead, and the local trades unions, the Irish Citizen Army, the Cumann na mBan, the Fianna, and as many of the citizens of Dublin as desired to do so. The Fintan Lalor Pipe Band, connected with the Irish Transport and General Workers Union, were to play the Dead March. And there was to be a firing party of the Irish Volunteers who were to use the rifles that had so soon been the cause of bloodshed.

I spent all the day of the funeral making wreaths. The funeral was not to take place till the evening so as to permit all who wished to attend to do so. The Fianna boys went round to the different florists asking for flowers to make wreaths to place on the graves of the dead. And they were richly rewarded. Every florist they went to gave bunches and bunches of their best flowers, and these the boys brought to Madame's house. Madame and I, and two or three other girls, worked continually all during the afternoon turning the flowers into wreaths. When we had finished we had seventeen glorious big wreaths. Just before six we piled into an automobile, some of the boys in Gaelic costume stood on the running board. The saffron and green of the kilts and the many wreaths made quite an artistic dash of color when we arrived at Beresford Place to have our place assigned to us.

The bodies of the five victims were removed from the Cathedral and placed in the hearses. Behind each one walked the chief mourners. Much interest was aroused by the sight of a soldier in the English uniform, who marched, weeping openly, after one of the hearses. He had joined the English Army and had promised to protect the English King, and now the soldiers of that king had shot and killed his innocent defenseless mother.

Dublin was profoundly moved as the funeral cortege passed through the city. Thousands upon thousands marched to the cemetery after the hearses, and thousands more lined the streets. They were attesting their sympathy with the families of the dead, and their realization that England still intended to rule Ireland with the rifle and the bullet.

The firing party, as they marched after the hearses with their rifles reversed, excited much comment. The people contrasted the difference in the treatment accorded the Nationalists when they had a gun-running, with that accorded the Ulster gun-runners. And they knew once more that England would kill and destroy them rather than permit them to have the means to protect their lives and to fight for their liberties.

The authorities were aware of the feeling aroused in the people by the killing of the unarmed women and men, and to prevent any further disturbance they confined the soldiers to their barracks that evening. Still the feeling against "The King's Own Scottish Borderers" (the regiment that had done the shooting) ran so high that the entire regiment was secretly sent away from Dublin.

III

ABOUT one week later, while the people were still incensed at the shooting, England went to war. Almost immediately she issued an appeal to the Irish to join her army. Later she appealed to them to avenge the shooting of the citizens of Catholic Belgium. Because her memory was short, or perhaps because her need was so great she chose to ignore the fact that English soldiers had but shortly shot down and killed the unarmed citizens of Catholic Dublin. But Dublin did not forget.

The Irish Citizen Army distinguished itself when John Redmond and Mr. Asquith, who was then Prime Minister, came over to Dublin shortly after the outbreak of the war. They came to hold a recruiting meeting in the Mansion House. It was supposed to be a public meeting at which the Prime Minister and the Irish Parliamentary Leader would appeal to the citizens of Dublin to enlist in the British Army; yet no one was let in without a card of

THE UNBROKEN TRADITION

admission. A cordon of soldiers were drawn across both ends of the street in which the Mansion House was situated, at Nassau Street and at St. Stephen's Green. No one could pass these cordons without presenting the card and being subjected to a close scrutiny by the local detectives. This was to make sure that no objectionable person could get in to the meeting and make a row. But the Nationalists of Dublin had no intention of going to the meeting; there was to be another one that would give them more pleasure.

A monster demonstration had been decided upon by the Irish Citizen Army to prove to Mr. Asquith, and through him to England, that the mass of the Dublin people were against recruiting for the British Army. They mustered outside of Liberty Hall. The speakers, amongst whom was Sean Mac Dermott who was there to represent the Irish Volunteers, were on a lorry guarded by members of the Irish Citizen Army armed with rifles and fixed bayonets; a squad similarly armed guarded the front and the rear. They were determined that there would be no arrest of anti-recruiters that night.

They marched around the city, the crowd

swelling as they went, and they stopped at the "Traitors' Arch" (the popular name for the Memorial to the Irish soldiers who fell in the Boer War), at St. Stephen's Green, two blocks away from where the recruiting meeting was being held. As speaker after speaker denounced recruiting, and denounced England, and Redmond, and Asquith, feeling surged higher and higher until it reached a climax when James Connolly called on those present to declare for an Irish Republic. Cheers burst from thousands of throats and a forest of hands appeared in the air as they declared for a Republic. We were told afterwards that the recruiting meeting had to stop till the anti-recruiters stayed their cheering.

The armed men of the Irish Citizen Army resumed the march first to make sure that none would be molested. Down Grafton Street they went and halted again beside the old House of Parliament, where Jim Larkin called on them to raise their right hands and pledge themselves never to join the British Army. Every one present did so. Then, whistling and singing Nationalist marching tunes and anti-recruiting songs, they marched back to Liberty Hall and dispersed. As a result of

Asquith's meeting, or because of the Irish Citizen Army meeting, only six men joined the British Army next day.

Midnight mobilizations were a feature of the Irish Citizen Army. They served a twofold purpose. They taught the men to be ready whenever called upon, and were a great source of annoyance to the police. At every mobilization of the Irish Citizen Army a squad of police and detectives were detailed by the authorities to follow and report all the movements. One midnight the men mobilized at Liberty Hall; they were divided into two bodies, the attacking and the defending. They marched to the North side of the city, one body going across the canal, and the other remaining behind to prevent the entrance of the attackers. The battle lasted two hours. It was a bitter winter's night and the police were on duty all the time as they did not dare to leave, for there was no telling what the Irish Citizen Army might be up to.

After the men had completed their evolutions around the bridge they formed ranks and marched round the city, the police following them. They stopped at Emmet Hall, Inchicore, for refreshments. There they had a song

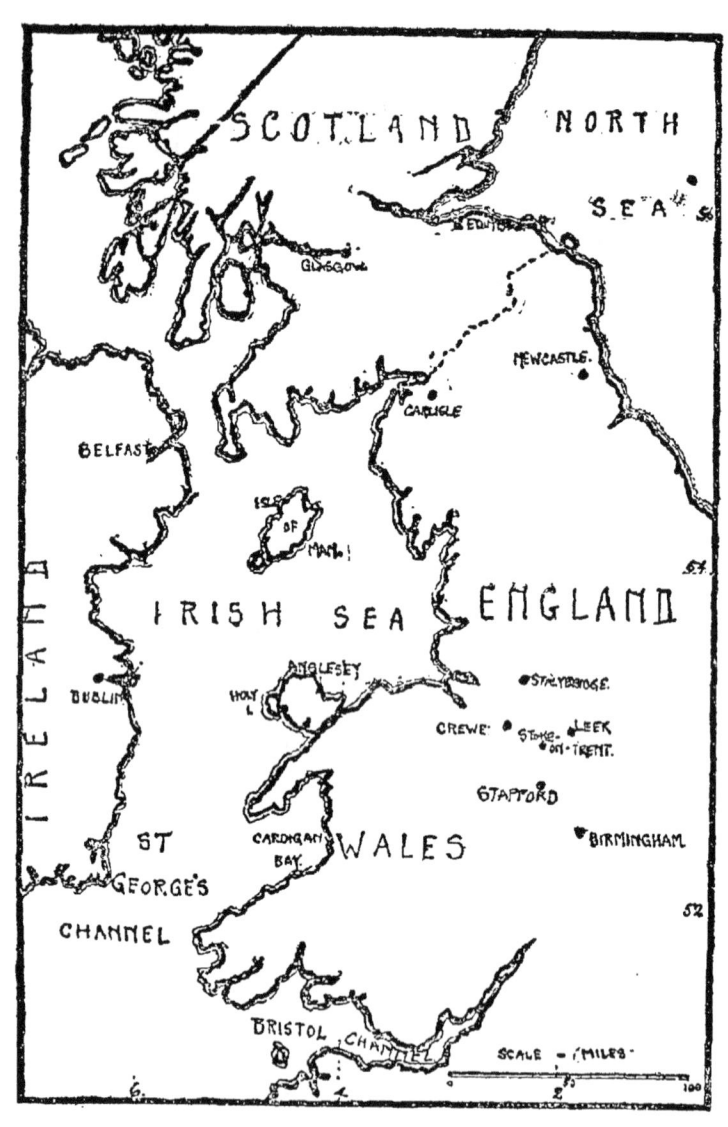

Illustrating journey from Belfast to Leek.
See pages 54-71

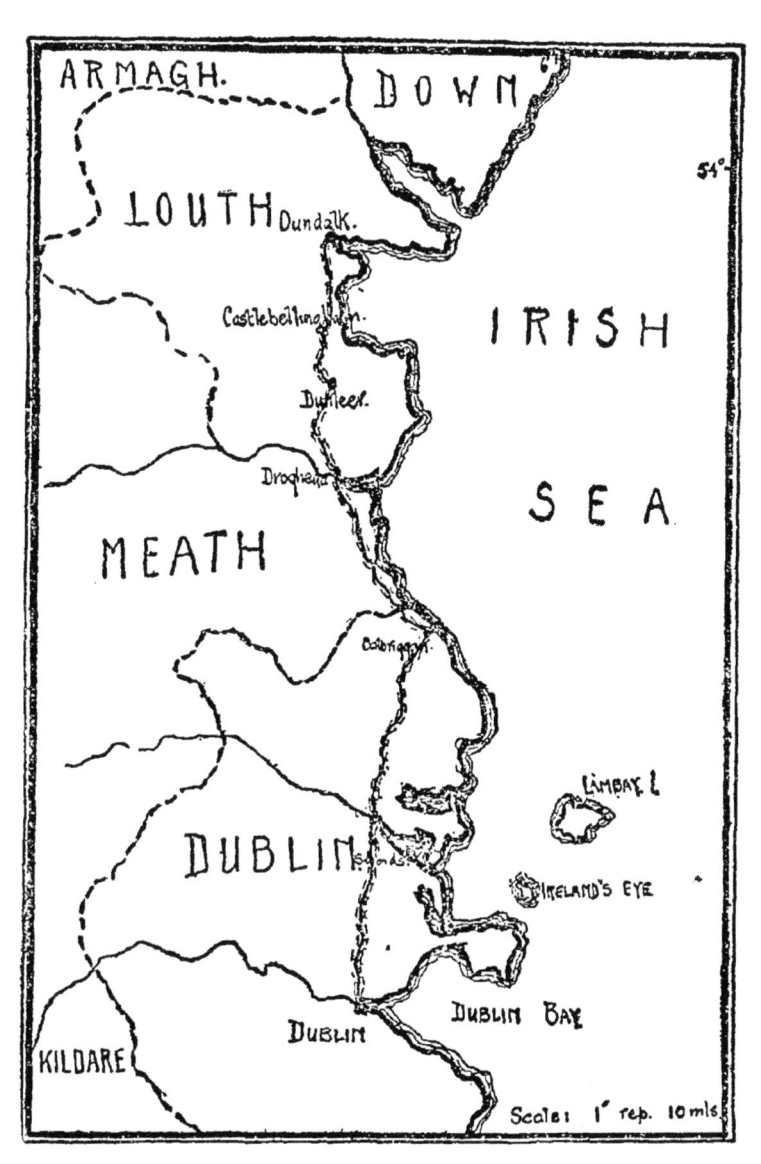

Illustrating the journey from Dundalk to Dublin.
See pages 142-163

24 THE UNBROKEN TRADITION

and dance, one chap remarking that the thought of the "peelers" (police) and the "G men" (detectives) outside in the cold added to the enjoyment. They broke up about six o'clock a. m. and marched back to Liberty Hall followed by the disheartened, miserable, frozen police.

There was another midnight mobilization later on. Announcements were made publicly that on this occasion the Irish Citizen Army would attack Dublin Castle, the center of English Government in Ireland for 600 years. The thought of such a deed never fails to fire the imagination of an Irish Nationalist. A favorite phrase of one of the officers of the Irish Citizen Army, Commandant Sean Connolly, was, "One more rush, boys, and the Castle is ours." He was in command of the body that attacked the Castle on Easter Monday. It was while calling on his men to rush the Castle that he received a bullet through his brain, thus achieving his lifelong dream of dying for Ireland while attacking the Castle.

One other mobilization which took place at midnight some time before the Rising was a disappointment, perhaps because it was unofficial. One of the Irish Citizen Army men heard that a number of rifles were stored in a place near Finglass. He knew the whereabouts and whispered the news amongst his comrades. A number of them decided to make a raid on the place and capture the rifles. They started out at midnight, marched twenty miles before morning, but, unfortunately, the rifles had been removed before they arrived. They were disappointed but not downhearted; such things they considered part of the day's work.

They had another disappointment which was more amusing, at least our men could laugh at it when a few days were past. There was in Dublin a body of men called the Home Defense Corps. They wore a greenish gray uniform and on their sleeves an armlet with the letters "G. R." in red—abbreviations for Georgius Rex. They were called the "Gorgeous Wrecks" by the Dubliners. They were mainly men past the military age who had registered their willingness to fight the Germans when they invaded England, Scotland, or Ireland. These men paraded the streets of Dublin making a fine show with their uniforms and rifles, especially the rifles. Some of the Irish Citizen Army thought those rifles too good to be left in the hands of "those old ones" and followed them on a march to find out where the rifles were kept. When our men came back they gathered a number of their friends together; after a short talk away they went for the rifles. It was done in quite a military manner; sentries and pickets were placed, the building surrounded and entered. Several made their way to the room where the rifles were kept and opened the windows to hand the rifles to the eager hands outside. Their plan was to march home with them quite openly as if returning from a route march.

The leader of the band was well known for his lurid and swift flow of language. Suddenly bursting out, he surpassed all his previous efforts and completely staggered the men around him—they beheld him examining one of the rifles. It was complete in every detail, just like an army rifle, but on lifting it it was easy to know that it was a very clever imitation. The men were heartbroken and disgusted, but they brought several of the rifles away with them to show their officers what the "Gorgeous Wrecks" were going to fight the Germans with. During a raid by the Dublin police in a well-known house one of these rifles was taken away by them. How long it took them to realize its uselessness we do not know as it was never returned.

IV

Towards the end of 1915 the hearts of the Irish Citizen Army beat high, when they were summoned one night for special business. One by one they were called into a room where their Commandant, James Connolly, and his Chief of Staff, Michael Mallin, were seated at a table. They were bound on their word not to reveal anything they should hear until the time came. Something like the following conversation took place:

"Are you willing to fight for Ireland?"

"Yes."

"It might mean your death."

"No matter."

"Are you ready to fight to-morrow if asked?"

"Whenever I'm wanted."

"Do you think we ought to fight with the few arms we've got?"

"Why wait? England can get millions to our one."

"It might mean a massacre."

"In God's name let us fight, we've been waiting long enough."

"The Irish Volunteers might not come out with us. Are you still ready?"

"What matter? We can put up a good fight."

"Then in God's name hold yourself ready. The Day is very near."

To the eternal credit of the Irish Citizen Army be it recorded that only one man shirked that night.

Then on top of this glorious happening came the attempted raid on Liberty Hall by the police. That morning I was in the office with my father when a man came from the printer's shop and said, "Mr. Connolly, you're wanted downstairs." My father went downstairs. About five minutes later he came into the office again, took down a carbine, loaded it and filled his pockets with cartridges.

"What is it?" I asked. "Can I do anything?"

"Stay here, I'll need you," said my father and he left the office again. He was gone about five minutes when the door was banged open and the Countess de Markievicz burst into the office.

"Where's Mr. Connolly?" she demanded excitedly. "Where's Mr. Connolly? They're raiding the Gaelic press—the place is surrounded with soldiers."

"He left here five minutes ago," I said. "He took his carbine with him and told me to remain here as he would need me."

She ran out again. In a few minutes I heard her and my father coming back along the corridor. She was talking excitedly and my father was laughing.

They came into the office—he took down a sheaf of papers and commenced signing them. They called for instant mobilization of the Irish Citizen Army. They were to report at Liberty Hall with full equipment at once.

"Well, Nora," said my father. "It looks as if we were in for it and as if they were going to force our hands. Fill up these orders as I sign them. I want two hundred and fifty."

I busied myself filling in these orders. The Countess began to help me—suddenly she stopped and cried out, "But, Mr. Connolly, I haven't my pistol on me."

"Never mind, Madame," said my father. "We'll give you one."

"Give it to me now," she said. "So my mind will be easy."

She was given a large Mauser pistol. Just then a picket came running in. He saluted and said, "They've left the barracks, sir." He was referring to the police. A line of our pickets had been stationed reaching from the barracks to Liberty Hall; their duty was to report any move they might see made by the police. In that way no sooner had a body of police left the barracks than word was sent along the line and in less than three minutes Liberty Hall was aware of it.

"Now, Madame," said my father when the picket had gone. "Come along, we'll be ready for them. Finish those, Nora, and come down to me with them."

I finished them and went down to the Co-operative shop. Behind the counter stood my father with his carbine laid along it; beside him Madame, and outside the counter was Miss Moloney taking the safety catch from off her automatic. I gave the batch of orders to my father; he called one of the men who stood in the doorway, and said, "Get these around at once." The man saluted and went away. Just then another picket came in and said, "They will be here in a minute, sir, they've just crossed the bridge."

"Very well," said my father, and the men went away.

Miss Moloney then told me that some policemen had come in and had attempted to search the store, and that she had sent word to Mr. Connolly through the men in the printing shop, which was back of the Coöperative shop; and then busied herself resisting the search. One policeman had a batch of papers in his hands when my father came in. He saw at once what was going forward, drew his automatic pistol, pointed it at the policeman and said:

"Drop them or I'll drop you."

The policeman dropped them. My father then asked what he wanted. He said they had come to confiscate any copies of *The Gael, The Gaelic Athlete, Honesty* or *The Spark* that might be on the premises.

"Have you a search warrant?" asked my father. This was a bluff, because under the Defense of the Realm Act any house may be searched on suspicion; but it worked; the policeman said he had none.

"Go and get one," said my father, "or you'll not search here."

The police went away; and it was then that my father had come back to the office to sign the mobilization papers.

Shortly afterwards there came into the shop an Inspector of the police, four plain-clothes men and two policemen in uniform. I was behind the counter at this time.

"I am Inspector Banning," said the Inspector.

"What do you want?" asked my father.

"We have come to search for, and confiscate any, of the suppressed papers we may find here."

"Where's your warrant?" asked my father.

"I have it here," said the Inspector.

"Read it," said my father.

The Inspector read the warrant—it was to the effect that all shops and newsvendors were to be searched, and all copies of the suppressed newspapers confiscated.

"Well," said my father when the Inspector had finished reading. "This is the shop up to this door,"—pointing to one behind him,—"beyond this door is Liberty Hall, and through

34 THE UNBROKEN TRADITION

this door you will not go. Go ahead and search."

"We have no desire to enter Liberty Hall," said the Inspector.

"I don't doubt you," said my father, whereat we all grinned.

At an order from the Inspector one of the policemen began to search around the place where the papers were kept. He looked at my father standing in the doorway with his carbine, and for a moment we thought he was going to rush him. Perhaps visions of stripes danced before him; but, at an order from his superior he went on with his work. It was a good thing for him that he did so, as there were the best of shots present, with less than ten paces between him and them.

"There is nothing here," he said at last to the Inspector. (We had made sure there would not be.) And then they all left the shop.

In the meantime, a series of strange sights were to be seen all over the city. The mobilization orders had gone forth and the men were answering them. Women in the fashionable shopping districts were startled by the sight of men, with their faces still grimed with the dust of their work, tearing along at a breakneck speed, a rifle in one hand and a bandolier in the other.

Out from the ships where they were working; from the docks; out of the factories; in from the streets,—racing, panting, with eager faces and joyful eyes they trooped into Liberty Hall. Joyful because they believed the call had come at last.

No obstacle was great enough to prevent their answering the order. One batch were working in a yard overlooking a canal. A man appeared at the door, whistled to one of the men and gave him a sign.

"Come on, boys, we're needed," cried one and made for the door. The foreman, thinking it was a strike, closed the door. Nothing daunted they swarmed the walls, jumped into the canal, swam across, ran to their homes for their rifles and equipment and arrived at Liberty Hall, wet and happy. Another batch were busy with a concrete column and had just got it to the critical period, where one must not stop working or it hardens and cannot be used, when the mobilizer appeared at the door and gave them the news. Down went the tools and out they went through the gate in the twinkling of an eye.

All day long the men were arriving at Liberty Hall. Tense excitement prevailed amongst the crowds that came thronging outside the Hall. A guard was placed at the great front door, another at the head of the wide staircase and the rest were confined to the guard room. This guard room had a great fascination for me. The men were sitting on forms around an open fire; ranged along the walls were their rifles, and hanging above them their bandoliers; at the butts of the rifles were their haversacks containing the rest of their equipment; all was so arranged that when they received an order each man would be armed and equipped within a minute, and there would be no confusion or delay. When I first went in the men were singing, with great gusto, this Citizen Army marching tune:

> We've got guns and ammunition, we know how to use them well,
> And when we meet the Saxon we'll drive them all to Hell.
> We've got to free our country, and avenge all those who fell,
>   And our cause is marching on.
>   Glory, glory to old Ireland,
>   Glory, glory to our sireland,
> Glory to the memory of those who fought and fell,
>   And we still keep marching on.

THOMAS J. CLARKE

I knew then what was meant by sniffing a battle. I did not want to leave that room. The atmosphere thrilled me so that I regarded with impatience the men and women who were going about the Hall attending to the regular business of the Union, and not in the least perturbed by all the military display. "Business as usual," one chap remarked to me as I stood watching them all.

I did not stand long, for a Citizen Army man came to me and said, "You're wanted in No. 7 by Mr. Connolly." No. 7 was my father's office. When I got there my father said, "Nora, I have a carbine up at Surrey House and a bandolier. It is in my room." He then told me where. "I want you to get one of the scouts, who are always at Madame's house, to put the bandolier on and over it my heavy overcoat. Tell him to swing the rifle over his shoulder and come down here with it as if he were mobilizing. Get him here as soon as you can. I'll be staying here all night," he added.

I started off immediately for Rathmines where Surrey House, Countess de Markievicz's residence, is situated. On my way I met one of the scouts who was going there. When I told him my errand he offered to be the one

38 THE UNBROKEN TRADITION

to bring the things back to Liberty Hall. When we reached the house, I went to the room, found the things which my father wanted and brought them down to the scout. He had just put them on when Madame called from the kitchen and asked me to have some tea. Of course I said I would have some. While I was waiting to be served she said to me, "What do you think is going to happen? I am going down to Liberty Hall immediately to take my turn of standing guard. By-the-way, what do you think of my uniform?"

She stepped out into the light where I could get a good view of her. She had on a dark green woolen blouse trimmed with brass buttons, dark green tweed knee breeches, black stockings and high heavy boots. As she stood she was a good advertisement for a small arms factory. Around her waist was a cartridge belt, suspended from it on one side was a small automatic pistol, and on the other a convertible Mauser pistol-rifle. Hanging from one shoulder was a bandolier containing the cartridges for the Mauser, and from the other was a haversack of brown canvas and leather which she had bought from a man, who had got it from a soldier, who in turn had brought it back from the front; originally it had belonged to a German soldier. I admired her whole outfit immensely. She was a fine military figure.

"You look like a real soldier, Madame," I said, and she was as pleased as if she had received the greatest compliment.

"What is your uniform like?" she asked.

"Somewhat similar," I answered. "Only I have puttees and my boots have plenty of nails in the soles. I intend wearing my scout blouse and hat."

"This will be my hat," she said and showed me a black velour hat with a heavy trimming of coque feathers. When she put it on she looked like a Field Marshal; it was her best hat.

"What arms have you?" she then asked.

"A .32 revolver and a Howth rifle."

"Have you ammunition for them?"

"Some. Perhaps enough."

I then turned to the scout who was to carry my father's rifle and bandolier to Liberty Hall, and said, "We'd better go now." Saying "Slán libh" ("Health with ye") we left the room. On our way to the door we heard a heavy rap at it. I ran forward and opened it. Judge of my surprise to see two detectives standing outside.

"What do you want?" I asked.

"The Countess de Markievicz."

"Wait," I said and closed the door.

Running back to the room I said, "Madame, there are two detectives at the door. They say they want you."

All the boys looked to their revolvers, and the boy who had my father's rifle said, "I hope I'll be able to get these down to Mr. Connolly."

Madame went into the hall and lit a small glimmer of light. The boys remained in the darkened background, and I opened the door.

The detectives came just inside of the door.

"What do you want with me?" asked Madame.

"We have an order to serve on you, Madame," said one of them.

"What is it about?" asked Madame.

"It is an order under one of the regulations of the Defense of the Realm Act, prohibiting you from entering that part of Ireland called Kerry."

"Well," said Madame. "Is that to prevent me from addressing the meeting to-morrow night in Tralee?" Madame was advertised to speak at a meeting to organize a company of boy scouts the following day in the town of Tralee, County Kerry.

"I don't know, Madame," he answered.

"What will happen to me if I refuse to obey that order and go down to Kerry to-morrow?" asked Madame. "Will I be shot?"

"Ah, now, Madame, who'd want to shoot you? You wouldn't want to shoot one of us, would you, Madame?" said the detective who was doing all the talking.

"But I would," cried Madame. "I'm quite prepared to shoot and be shot at."

"Ah, now, Madame, you don't mean that. None of us want to die yet: we all want to live a little longer."

"If you want to live a little longer," said a voice from out of the darkness, "you'd better not be coming here. We're none of us very fond of you, and you make fine big targets."

"We'll be going now, Madame," said the detective. As he stepped out through the door he turned and said, "You'll not be thinking of going to Kerry, Madame, will you?"

"Good-by," said Madame cordially. "Remember, I'm quite prepared to shoot and be shot at."

42 THE UNBROKEN TRADITION

"Well," she said as the door closed. "What am I going to do now? I want to go and defy them. How can I do it? I'm so well known—but I'm under orders. Perhaps Mr. Connolly wouldn't allow me to go anyway. I'll go down and talk it over with him. Wait a minute, Nora, and we'll all be down together."

On our way down a brilliant idea, as I thought, struck me. "Write your speech out, Madame, make it as seditious and treasonable as possible. Send some one down to Tralee to deliver it for you at the meeting. In that way, the meeting will be held, your speech delivered, and the authorities will not be able to arrest you on that charge."

"I was just thinking of that and who I could send down. But I'll decide nothing till I see Mr. Connolly," said Madame.

We met my father at the top of the staircase in Liberty Hall.

"What do you think, Mr. Connolly," cried Madame. "I've received an internment order or rather an order prohibiting me from going down to Tralee. What am I going to do about it? Shall I go or shall I obey the order."

"Did you bring the carbine and bandolier?" asked my father turning to me.

"Yes," I answered. "Harry has them."

"No, Madame," said my father. "You cannot go down to Tralee. If you make the attempt you will probably be arrested at some small station on the way, and sentenced to some months in jail. You are too valuable to be a prisoner at a time like this; I'll have need of you. If the authorities follow up their action of to-day we may be in the middle of things to-night or to-morrow; who knows? No, you must stay here. You are more important than the meeting."

"Should I send some one in my place, then?" asked Madame.

"That is for you to decide, though I think it would be a good thing."

"Whom will I send?" asked Madame.

"Send some one who cannot be victimized in case our hands are not forced; some one who is already victimized. Why not ask Mairé Perolz?"

"The very girl!" said Madame. "You can always pick out the right person."

"You had better get hold of Perolz, then," said my father. "Tell her what you want her to do and write out your speech. We'll relieve you of guard duty to-night, and promise you that if things look lively we'll get word to you in time."

Madame left the Hall, and when I returned to her house a few hours later, she was busy writing out her speech. I sat down in the room and from time to time she read me out parts of it. It certainly was seditious and treasonable. She wrote on for quite some time after that and then with a sigh of satisfaction she said, "I have it finished. Perolz will come for it in the morning—she will take an early train."

Perolz had come and gone before I came down in the morning, but when she returned a few days later, I heard the whole story of her adventure, told in her own inimitable way.

She had traveled down to Limerick Junction accompanied by a very polite, attentive detective, whose company she dispensed with there by leaving the carriage she was in at the very last minute, and taking a seat in another. Hers was not a case of impersonation, for the Countess de Markievicz is very tall and rather fair while Mairé Perolz is of medium height and has red hair. She is very quick-witted and nimble of her tongue, never at a loss for what to do or for what to say.

POBLACHT NA H EIREANN.
THE PROVISIONAL GOVERNMENT
OF THE
IRISH REPUBLIC
TO THE PEOPLE OF IRELAND.

IRISHMEN AND IRISHWOMEN: In the name of God and of the dead generations from which she receives her old tradition of nationhood, Ireland, through us, summons her children to her flag and strikes for her freedom.

Having organised and trained her manhood through her secret revolutionary organisation, the Irish Republican Brotherhood, and through her open military organisations, the Irish Volunteers and the Irish Citizen Army, having patiently perfected her discipline, having resolutely waited for the right moment to reveal itself, she now seizes that moment, and, supported by her exiled children in America and by gallant allies in Europe, but relying in the first on her own strength, she strikes in full confidence of victory.

We declare the right of the people of Ireland to the ownership of Ireland, and to the unfettered control of Irish destinies, to be sovereign and indefeasible. The long usurpation of that right by a foreign people and government has not extinguished the right, nor can it ever be extinguished except by the destruction of the Irish people. In every generation the Irish people have asserted their right to national freedom and sovereignty; six times during the past three hundred years they have asserted it in arms. Standing on that fundamental right and again asserting it in arms in the face of the world, we hereby proclaim the Irish Republic as a Sovereign Independent State, and we pledge our lives and the lives of our comrades-in-arms to the cause of its freedom, of its welfare, and of its exaltation among the nations.

The Irish Republic is entitled to and hereby claims the allegiance of every Irishman and Irishwoman. The Republic guarantees religious and civil liberty, equal rights and equal opportunities to all its citizens, and declares its resolve to pursue the happiness and prosperity of the whole nation and of all its parts, cherishing all the children of the nation equally and oblivious of the differences carefully fostered by an alien government, which have divided a minority from the majority in the past.

Until our arms have brought the opportune moment for the establishment of a permanent National Government, representative of the whole people of Ireland and elected by the suffrages of all her men and women, the Provisional Government, hereby constituted, will administer the civil and military affairs of the Republic in trust for the people.

We place the cause of the Irish Republic under the protection of the Most High God, Whose blessing we invoke upon our arms, and we pray that no one who serves that cause will dishonour it by cowardice, inhumanity, or rapine. In this supreme hour the Irish nation must, by its valour and discipline and by the readiness of its children to sacrifice themselves for the common good, prove itself worthy of the august destiny to which it is called.

Signed on behalf of the Provisional Government.

THOMAS J. CLARKE.
SEAN Mac DIARMADA.   THOMAS MacDONAGH.
P. H. PEARSE.   EAMONN CEANNT.
JAMES CONNOLLY.   JOSEPH PLUNKETT.

THE PROCLAMATION OF THE PROVISIONAL GOVERNMENT ISSUED AT THE G. P. O., ON MONDAY, APRIL 24TH, 1917.

She was met at Tralee station by a guard of honor from the local Cumann na mBan (women's organization), Irish Volunteers, and intending boy scouts. They had never seen the Countess de Markievicz and consequently did not know that it was not she who had arrived. Although Mairé told me that she almost lost her composure when she heard one of the girls say, "She isn't a bit like her photograph."

She was escorted to the hotel. When she arrived there she said to the officers of the organization, "I am not Madame Markievicz. She received an order last night prohibiting her from entering Kerry. Things were looking lively in Dublin and Madame was needed. She wrote out her speech and I am to deliver it for her. In that way the meeting will be held and Madame's speech will be delivered, and Madame will still be able to do useful work. There is no need to let the public know till to-night."

The officers agreed that it would be best to keep the knowledge of the non-arrival of Madame from the public and the police. Just then the proprietor of the hotel came to the door and said, "Madame, there are two policemen downstairs and they want your registration form at once." Under the Defense of the Realm Act every one entering an hotel, or boarding or lodging house is required to fill in a form declaring his name, address, occupation, and intended destination. This rule was most rigidly enforced by the police authorities.

"Can't they wait till I get a cup of tea?" asked Mairé.

"No. They said they would wait and take it back to the station with them."

"Very well," said Mairé. "Give it to me."

She filled out the form something like this, neglecting the minor details.

>   *Name:*—Mairé Perolz.
>   *Address:*—No fixed address—vagrant.
>   *Age:*—20?
>   *Occupation:*—None.
>   *Nationality:*—Irish.

She then gave it to the proprietor who took it away. From the window they watched the policemen carrying it to the police station, apparently very much absorbed in it. They returned shortly and asked to see the lady. When they came in to the room they still carried the registration form.

"You haven't filled in this form satisfactorily, Madame," said one. "You must have some fixed address and some occupation."

"No indeed," said Mairé. "I live on my wits."

"And you are a Russian subject."

"How do you make that out, in the name of God?" asked Mairé.

"You are married to a Russian Count."

"First news I've heard of it," said Mairé. "Now listen here, I've filled that form out correctly and you'll have to be satisfied with it. I'll not fill out another."

They accepted the form at last. That night Mairé delivered Madame's speech, told why Madame could not be present, then added a little anti-recruiting speech of her own which evoked great applause. The next day she returned home in great spirits at having once more helped to outwit the police.

V

ABOUT this time the Executive of the Cumann na mBan (women's organization) in Dublin were having trouble in procuring First Aid and Hospital supplies. I suggested that being a Northerner and having a Northern accent, I could probably get them in Belfast. I knew that a number of loyalist nursing corps were in existence in that city, and thought that by letting it be inferred that I belonged to one of them, the loyalist shopkeepers would have no hesitation in selling me the supplies, and in all probability would let me have them at cost price. And that is exactly what happened. I purchased as many of the different articles as I needed and at less than half the price paid in Dublin.

While in Dublin I had visited the Employment Bureau in the Volunteer Headquarters. Its business was to find employment for Irishmen and boys who were liable for military service. Under the Military Service Act every man or boy over eighteen, residing in England or Scotland since the preceding August, was required to report himself for service in the British Army. The Bureau found employment in most cases for those who preferred to serve in the Irish Republican Army and had come to Ireland to await the call. Of course, it was impossible to find jobs for them all; but those who had not received jobs were busy on the work of making ammunition and hand grenades for the Irish Republican Army. The greater number of them had to camp out during the miserable months of February and March, in the Dublin Mountains, so that too great a drain would not be placed on their slender resources.

On my return to Belfast at a meeting of the Cumann na mBan I suggested that we send hampers of foodstuffs down to those boys and men in Dublin. The suggestion was taken up with great gusto, and the members were divided into different squads; a butter squad, a bacon squad, a tea, a sugar, oatmeal, cheese, and tinned goods squad; and they were to solicit all their friends for these articles. They were then to be sent on to the different camps in Dublin to help on the fight. Since we had done so well on the foodstuffs I thought it would be as well to ask the men and boys in Belfast for cigarettes and tobacco. I set about collecting on the Saturday on which we intended sending away the first hamper of food. I was so successful that I was unable to return home for lunch before half-past three.

When I arrived home my sister met me at the door and said there was a man in the parlor who wanted to see me, and that he had been waiting since noon. I went into the room and saw one of my Dublin friends.

"Why, hello, Barney," I said. "What brings you here?"

He told me that there was some work before me and that he had the instructions. With this he handed me a letter. I recognized my father's handwriting on the envelope. The letter merely said:

"*Dear Nora*, The bearer will tell you what we want you to do. I have every confidence in your ability.
"Your father,
"JAMES CONNOLLY."

"What are we to do?" I asked turning to Barney.

"Liam Mellowes is to be deported to-morrow morning to England and we are to go there and bring him back."

"Sounds like a big job," I said. "What are the plans?"

"These are some of them," he answered showing me several pages closely written. "Some one will bring the final instructions from Dublin to-night."

The plan in the rough was that the messenger, being on the first glance uncommonly like Liam Mellowes, was to go to the place where he was interned and visit him. While he was visiting he was to change clothes with Liam Mellowes and stay behind, while Liam came out to me. We were then to make all speed to the station and lose no time in returning to Dublin.

Liam Mellowes had received, some time previously, an order from the military authorities to leave Ireland. This was because of his many activities as an organizer for the Irish Volunteers—as the order had it, because he was prejudicial to recruiting. He refused to obey and had been arrested. He was now to be forcibly deported. As Mellowes was absolutely essential to the plans for the Rising, being Officer in charge of the operations in the

West of Ireland, the attempt to bring him back from England was decided upon.

While waiting for the messenger to bring the final instructions from Dublin I sent out word to some of the Cumann na mBan girls that I should like to see them. When they came I told them that I had received an order that necessitated my going to Dublin; and that I should not be able to assist them in sending away the hampers. I gave them the money that I had collected for the cigarettes and tobacco, and they said they would see that everything went away all right. It was with great surprise and delight that the "refugees," as we called them, received the hampers a few days later.

VI

AFTER the girls left I fell to studying the instructions. The main idea was to go in as zig-zag a course as possible to our objective. My father had made out a list of the best possible places to break our journey. On one sheet of paper in Eamonn Ceannt's handwriting continued the plan; and on another, in Sean mac Diarmuida's, was a list of people with their addresses in England or Scotland, to whom we could go for safe hiding, if we found we were being followed by detectives.

Shortly after seven that evening Miss Moloney arrived at our house. She brought us a message from Dublin. It was to the effect that it was not yet known to what place Liam Mellowes was to be deported, but we were to go on our journey, and when we arrived at Birmingham, there would be a message waiting us there with the desired information. All that was known was that Liam Mellowes was to be deported to some town in the South of England.

There was a boat leaving for Glasgow that night at eleven forty-five. We decided to go on it; it was called the theatrical boat, because it was on this boat many theatrical companies left Belfast; we thought we would not be noticed among the throng. I was to ask for all the tickets at the railway stations, as my accent is not easily placed.

On Sunday morning I went up on deck expecting to be almost the first one there; Barney, however, was there before me. He said we would be in Glasgow shortly. I went below for my suitcase. When I came up on deck again I saw that we were nearer shore and that we were slowing up. I asked a steward if we should be off soon.

"No," he said. "We are slowing up here to put some cattle off."

"Will it take long?" I asked.

"About an hour."

"How far are we from Glasgow?" I then asked.

"Two or three miles."

"Can we get off here instead of waiting?"

"Nothing to prevent you," he said.

So Barney and I picked up our traps and, as soon as the gangway was fixed up for the

THE UNBROKEN TRADITION 55

cattle to disembark, we went down it and on to the quay.

We walked along as if we had been born there, although as a matter of fact, neither Barney nor I had been in that place before. After a few minutes we came to a street with tramway lines on it and decided to wait for a car. We boarded the first car that came along. After riding in it for a long time we noticed that instead of approaching the city we seemed to be going farther away from it. We left the car at the next stop, and took another going in the opposite direction, and after riding for three-quarters of an hour arrived in Glasgow. We were more than pleased to think that if the police had noticed us when we went on the Glasgow boat at Belfast, and had sent on word for the Glasgow police to watch out for us, the boat would arrive without us.

Our next stop was to be Edinburgh. We went to the station and inquired when the Edinburgh train would be leaving. There was one leaving at eleven fifteen that would arrive in Edinburgh some time about one o'clock. We decided to go by it. Then we remembered that it was Sunday and that we had not been to Mass; also that if we went by that train it would be too late when we arrived at Edinburgh to attend. It was not quite ten o'clock then; if we could find a church nearby, we could go to Mass and still be in time for the train. But where was there a church? "Look, Barney," I cried suddenly. "Here's an Irish-looking guard. We'll ask him to direct us." We asked him and he told us that there was a Catholic church five minutes' walk away from the station, and directed us to it. It took us more than five minutes to get there, but we arrived in time and were back at the station before the Edinburgh train left.

We arrived at Edinburgh about one o'clock. We were very tired as we had not slept on the boat; and we were hungry for we had not eaten in our excitement at leaving the boat before the time. Our first thought was to find a place to eat; but it was Sunday in Scotland and we found no place open. After wandering around for some time, looking all about us, we decided to ask a policeman. He directed us to the Waverley Hotel, where we were given a good dinner. And when we told the waiter that we were only waiting till our train came due, and that we wanted a place to rest, he told us that we could stay in the room we were in. After dinner I found myself nodding and lay down on the couch. I must have fallen asleep almost instantly for it was dark when I awoke. Barney came in shortly afterwards. He had been looking up the trains he said and our train left at ten o'clock. It was about eight o'clock. We had something more to eat and left the hotel to go to the railway station.

To my great surprise when we came outside everything was dark. Not a light showed from any of the buildings, or from the street cars. Cabs and motors went by, and only for the shouting of the drivers and the blowing of the motor-horns we would have been run down when crossing the streets. We have no such war regulation of darkness in Ireland. We arrived at the station at last. We had to go down a number of steps to get to the gate, and if it was dark in the streets it was pitch blackness down there. I was not surprised at the number of people I met on the steps, as I thought it might be a usual rallying place, but I was surprised to hear them talking in whispers. We went down till we came to the gate—it was closed and there was a man on guard at it.

"Can we not get in?" I asked.

"Where are you going?"

"To Carlisle."

"It's not time for the Carlisle train yet."

"But can't we go in and take our seats?" I asked.

"No," he answered, and after that I could get no further response.

We waited awhile at the gate. I noticed that quite a few were given the same answers although they were not going to the same place. More time passed and I began to feel anxious; I was afraid that we would miss the train.

"What time is it now?" I asked, turning to Barney. As he could not see in the dark he lit a match. Instantly, as with one voice, every one around and on the steps shouted, "Put out that light." And the man at the gate howled, "What the H—— does that fool mean!" We were more than surprised; we did not know why we could not light a match.

Just after that a couple of soldiers came towards the gate. I could hear the rattle of their hob-nailed boots and see the rifles swung on their shoulders. They talked with the man at the gate for a few minutes, then saying, "All right," went up the steps again. This happened more than once. My eyes were accus-

THE UNBROKEN TRADITION

tomed to the darkness by now, and I could see a sergeant, with about twenty soldiers, coming down the steps. As they made for the gate I whispered to Barney, "Go close and listen to what the guard says to the sergeant." He went—and as the sergeant turned away, came back to me and picking up our bags said, "Come on." I followed without asking any questions. When we were out on the street Barney turned to me and said, "The guard told the sergeant to go to the other gate. We'll go to."

We followed the clacking sound of the soldiers' boots till we came to a big gate. It was evidently the gate used for vehicles. As we entered we were stopped by two guards who asked, "Where are you going?" "To Carlisle," I answered. They waved us inside. We walked down a long passageway. When we came to the train platforms, I asked a porter who was standing near:

"Where is the train for Carlisle?"

"There'll be no train to-night, Miss," he answered.

"But why?"

"Because, Miss," in a whisper, "the Zeppelins were seen only eight miles away, and a moving train would be a good mark for them."

"But they will not come here, will they?" I asked.

"They are headed this way, Miss, they may be here in half an hour."

"Then we can't get to Carlisle?"

"To tell you the truth, Miss," he said, "I don't think any train will run to-night, except the military train. Make up your mind you'll not get to Carlisle to-night."

"When is there a train in the morning?" I asked him then.

"There's one at eight-fifteen."

"Well, I suppose we'll go by that one," I said.

And so we left the station.

We went back to the hotel. We were startled for a second when the registration forms were handed to us; we hadn't decided on a name or address. I took the forms and filled them with a Belfast address, put the one for Barney in front of him, placing the pencil on the name so that he would know what to sign. After signing we were shown to our rooms. I went to bed immediately as I was completely tired out. I was roused from a heavy sleep

THE UNBROKEN TRADITION

by a knocking on the door, and a voice saying something I couldn't distinguish. I thought it was the "Boots" wakening me for breakfast, and turned over to finish my sleep. Some time later I was again wakened by a loud knocking on the door.

"Who is it?" I called out.

"Barney," was the answer.

"What is wrong?" I asked when I had opened the door.

"The manageress came to me," said Barney, "and said, 'Mr. Williams, go to your sister, I am afraid she is either dead or has fainted with the shock.'"

"What shock?" I asked, peering into the black darkness but failing to see anything.

"Nothing, only the Zeppelins have been dropping bombs all over the town."

"What!" I cried. "Zeppelins! You don't mean it. Have I slept through all their bombing?"

"You have," he said dryly. "The manageress wants all guests down in the parlor, so that in case this building is damaged, they'll all be near the street. Put something on and come down."

I put some clothes on me and went outside

the room. I could not see my own hand in front of me.

"Hold on to me," said Barney, "and I'll bring you downstairs. I know where the stairs are."

"All right," I said, making a clutch at where the voice was coming from.

"You'd better hold on to my back," said Barney. "That's the front of my shirt you've got."

I slid my hand around till I felt the suspenders at the back and held onto them. "Go ahead," I said, and we went. I tried to remember if the corridor was long or short, and if there were any turns from the stairs to my room, but I could not. Never have I walked along a corridor as long as that one seemed. After a bit I said, "Barney, are you sure you're going right? I don't remember it being as long as this." We were going very slowly, gingerly placing one foot after the other.

"We keep on," said Barney, "till we come to a turn and then between two windows are the stairs." And so we went on, but we came to no turning. We were feeling our way by placing our hands on the wall. At last, we felt an open space. "Ah," said Barney, "this

THE UNBROKEN TRADITION 63

must be the stairs." And although we did not feel the windows we cautiously stepped towards it. It was not the stairs and I felt curiously familiar with it. I stumbled over something on the floor and stooped to pick up—my shoe. We were back at my room! We did not know whether to laugh or to be annoyed. We began to laugh and Barney said, "Come on, I know the way back to my room and from there we'll find the stairs."

"Couldn't you strike a match?" I asked.

"We were warned not to, when the 'Boots' knocked on the door," said Barney. We went along the corridor till Barney found his room. From there he knew the turns of the corridor, and at last we found the stairs. Going down I asked, "How is it that we are meeting none of the people?"

"Because," said Barney, "they've been down since the first knock and you had to be wakened twice."

"I thought they were wakening me for breakfast," I said.

The stairs seemed to twist and turn, and at one of the turns I saw a figure standing at a window, near a landing as I thought.

"Are we going the right way down to the

64 THE UNBROKEN TRADITION

parlor?" I asked the figure, but received no reply.

"He's probably scared stiff and thinks he's in a safe place," said Barney. We reached the foot of the stairs and one of the men took us and led us towards the parlor. All the guests of the hotel were there huddled closely around the remains of the fire. I found a seat and sat down. There was very little talk. I could hear the guns going off very near. One of the women leaned toward me, and said, "You were rather long getting down. Did you faint—were you frightened?"

"No," I answered. "I slept through it all, until my brother came and wakened me."

"You lucky girl!" she exclaimed in heart-felt tones.

We sat there for about an hour. It was a silent hour inside, but from outside came the sound of running feet and hoarse excited voices. A motor car tore through the streets; it must have had its lamps lit, for some one yelled after it, "Put out those lights."

There was no sound of the Zeppelins again, but the people in the parlor kept silent. I felt that one word spoken would set all their nerves on edge. Suddenly there was a long drawn

"Oh!" followed by a thud. I could feel every one in the room quivering. All turned to the sound, but we could see nothing. Then we heard a man's voice say, "My boy has fainted." They ministered to him there in the darkness. A few minutes later a delicate looking lad, about twelve years old, was brought up to the circle round the fire. One of the women made room for him and he sat on the floor with his head resting on her knee. The manageress must have left the room during the excitement, for she returned then and said, "We will not be disturbed again, so we can go to bed and finish our sleep." The tension was lifted and we all began talking as we made our way to our rooms.

When I was going down the stairs next morning, I was amazed to see that the figure I had spoken to while trying to find my way, was a statue. The waiter told us, at breakfast, that some bombs had been dropped in the street back of the hotel. They had killed eight people, damaged one or two buildings, and made a hole large enough to hold the dining-room table. He also said that he had heard of a lot of other places, but that was the only one he had seen. We finished our breakfast

66 THE UNBROKEN TRADITION

in a hurry and left for the station. There we bought a paper to read the full account of the raid. But all the mention of it was:

"Zeppelins visited the East coast of Scotland last night. No damage done."

On the journey to Carlisle the carriage was so warm and the seats so soft that I became drowsy. I was about to yield when the other occupants of the carriage came over to my side and stared out of the windows. As the Zeppelins were still in my mind, I thought that this might be one of the places they had visited, and looked out of the window too. All I could see was a large field with brick buildings in the center, somewhat like factories, only they had sloping roofs made of glass. There were quite a crowd of men in the field. "That's a German Internment Camp," said one of the men. "There are over two thousand Germans there." The view of the camp started a conversation on the war which lasted till we reached Carlisle.

From Carlisle we were to go to Newcastle. On looking up the timetable we found that we could get a train in three-quarters of an hour. We then left the station, so that if the porters were questioned as to whether they had seen us or not they could say that we had left the station. In this way the trail would be broken and would give us all the more time till it was picked up again. The journey from Carlisle to Newcastle was not so long as the last one. On arriving there we again left the station and wandered about the town. We had so much more time there, and walked in and out of so many streets, crossed so many crossings, that my memory of Newcastle is very much blurred and confused. Before returning to the station we went into a restaurant and ate the first meal of our English trip.

Next we took tickets for Manchester, but did not go there. While we were on the train we decided that we had better go to Crewe. When the conductor came round for the tickets, we asked him if this train would take us to Crewe. No, he said, but if it was to Crewe we wanted to go he could change our tickets at the next stop, and there we would get a train for Crewe. The next station was Stalybridge, and there we took the train to Crewe, where we arrived at one-thirty a. m.

From Crewe we went to Birmingham. It was there we were to receive information as to where Captain Mellowes had been deported. We called at the address given to us and told who we were. Mr. Brown said that he had just received word that we were coming, but that was all. There was no news for us about the deportation. This was both amazing and puzzling; it was Tuesday and Captain Mellowes was to have been deported on the Sunday past. Why had we received no word—and what were we to do? There was nothing for us to do but wait. A hotel was recommended to us; we went there and registered as brother and sister. Our pose of being on a holiday compelled us to stay out all day as if sightseeing. Tuesday we visited all the principal buildings, Wednesday we walked all over the city. Thursday was a repetition of Wednesday. Friday, tired of each other's company, we went out separately, and each succeeded in losing the way, but managed to arrive back at the hotel for supper.

Not knowing the city we had not ventured out at night time, for like all other big cities in England, Birmingham was darkened at night-fall. But on Friday we went out. The streets seemed to be all alike to us, we could not tell one from the other. The corners of the curbstone were painted white, so as to glimmer faintly and warn pedestrians when they were approaching a crossing; policemen stood in the center of the crossing flashing a lamp attached to their belts, now a red light, now a green one. Trees, telegraph, telephone, and trolley poles were painted white to the level of the eyes. Not a light showed anywhere, not even at moving picture palaces; and as is usual in darkness all voices were subdued. I am sure it is at night time that the people of England realize most that they are at war.

Saturday came and still there was no news for us. We were not puzzled now. We were very anxious. Something must have gone wrong, we thought, or we would have had some word before now.

We changed our hotel as we felt that the people were becoming too interested in us. At the new hotel we registered as teachers on our way to Stratford-on-Avon, where the Shakespeare celebrations were in full swing. We left there in the morning, carried our suitcases to the station, and left them in the Left Luggage Office. Then we went to Mr. Brown again to find out if any word had come for us. There was a note for us there telling us to go to the

Midland Hotel. When we arrived there we met a young lady from Dublin. She had come over with the word. She gave us the address of Captain Mellowes, and told us to lose no time. We looked up the timetable and found that there were no trains going there on Sunday afternoon. We were in despair till our Birmingham friend told us he could hire a private motor car for us. He did so and we left Birmingham at one-thirty p. m.

We traveled all afternoon through what is known as the Black Country. We did not bother much with the scenery as we spent most of our time in giving each other instruction as to how to behave in different eventualities. We had hired the car to take us to Stoke-on-Trent. It was to return empty. We thought it would be a much safer plan if we could get the car to take us back to some big station on the line; thus instead of waiting at the local station for a train, apprehending every moment the discovery of Captain Mellowes' flight, we should be well on our way before it could be found out. I did not expect that there would be any trouble to get the chauffeur to bring us back. I figured that any money made on the return trip would be his, and a working man is always ready to make more money. But it must be done in such a way as not to arouse suspicion.

Secure in my figuring I spoke to the man. I said, "I want you to take us to the railway station at Stoke. I expect a friend there to pick us up." He nodded. It was dark when we drew up at the station. I said to the man, "Wait a minute till I see if my friend is there before we take out the things." Then I went into the station and walked in and out of the waiting rooms, up and down the platform, and asked a porter if there would be a train soon to Leek (our real objective). I returned and said to Barney, "He is not there," and to the man, "Have you any objections to going on to Leek? It is eight miles distant. There won't be a train for an hour, and I can have all my business in Leek done in that time." He said he would take us there. I then asked him if he were going straight back to Birmingham. He said he was. "If you can wait three-quarters of an hour, you can take us back down the line to one of the big stations, and be something in pocket. The trains are so irregular at small stations on Sundays." He said he could wait three-quarters of an hour.

When we arrived in Leek Barney and I jumped out of the car as if we knew every inch of the ground, although neither of us had been in the city before.

"Where are we going?" asked Barney.

"When in doubt go right," I said, and we turned to the right. This town was darkened too. After a few minutes' walk I stopped an old lady and asked her to direct us to the street I wanted. "Two streets up on the right," she replied. We found the place; it was an ordinary house and to our surprise there were no detectives watching it. We knocked at the door. A man opened it about six inches and peered at us.

"Well?" he questioned.

"We are friends of Captain Mellowes and heard he was staying here, so we stopped to see him," I said. "Is he in?"

"Come in till I take a look at you," he answered. After looking at us, "Come in here," he said, leading us to a room. "I'll go find him for you."

After a few minutes Captain Mellowes came into the room. He seemed surprised to see us, and was about to enter into a conversation with us when Barney said, "I've an important message to give you. Where's your room?"

"Come upstairs," said Captain Mellowes, rising at once.

They went upstairs. I could hear them moving about the room, and once in a while I heard something fall on the floor as if they were throwing different parts of their clothing to each other. After a few minutes' silence, I heard footsteps on the stairs and went out to the hall to be ready. Both came down the stairs, Captain Mellowes went forward and opened the door while I was saying "good-by" to Barney, who was remaining behind in the Captain's place. Barney left the house the following day; he took a train at the local station which ran to Crewe, and from there he made connections that brought him back to Ireland the day after the Captain's arrival.

Once outside the house, Captain Mellowes and myself wasted no time in getting to the car. I asked the man had we kept him long and he said we had been only half an hour. He started the car and away we went again. After three hours' ride we stopped at Stafford Station.

"Can you not go as far as Crewe?" I asked.

"No, Miss," he replied. "Crewe is altogether out of my direction."

"Very well," I said. "We'll leave here." We then left the car, gave the man his fee and entered the station. I took tickets for Crewe and found that we had only twenty minutes to wait. We arrived at Crewe about one a. m. and at one-thirty were in the train for Carlisle.

When we were near Carlisle the conductor came to collect the tickets; I asked him if Carlisle was the last stop.

"No," he said. "From there we go on to Glasgow without stopping."

"Oh," I said, "I didn't know that this train went to Glasgow. That's where we want to go. You had better make us out Excess Fare checks and we'll go on." He made them out; I paid them and he went out through the carriages. During this time Captain Mellowes was lying in the corner as if asleep.

In my list of "safe addresses" was one in Glasgow. When we arrived there next morning we made our way to that address, and there we stayed all day. During the day we managed to procure a clerical suit for Captain Mellowes, complete even to the breviary and umbrella. At eleven we took the train to Ardrossan; from there we could get a boat to Belfast. We had decided before leaving the house that we would travel as if we did not know each other. My accent was no longer needed, as a strong Irish accent was quite the thing for priests' clothing; but we were to keep each other in sight all the time.

That Captain Mellowes really looked the part was proved in the train. The porter lifted his cap to him, took his suitcase, and deferentially placed him in the seat next to me. There Captain Mellowes sat, his chin resting on his hands, which were supported by the umbrella, as if lost in holy meditations. Almost at the last moment, half-a-dozen North of Ireland cattle dealers tumbled into the carriage, shouting, laughing, and swearing. The porter had locked the door and the train had started before they realized what company they were in. A sudden silence fell on them all, they straightened themselves up, lifted their hats in salute to the priest, while questioning each other with their eyes. Then one lifted his cap again and turned to the rest as if to say, "I'm used to the company of priests," and addressed Captain Mellowes.

"Are you crossing to-night, Father?" he asked.

"I am," said Captain Mellowes.

"I hope we'll have a good night, Father."

"I hope so."

"I hear they caught a submarine up the Bangor Lough this morning; but I don't think there's any danger. Do you, Father?"

"I don't think so," said Captain Mellowes.

One dealer broke in then demanding to know that if there was no danger, why could they not insure the cattle they wanted to send across. Then each dealer tried to give his opinion at the same time. They became so excited, each one trying to get an audience at the same time, that they forgot all about the priest, and gave back word for word to each other. With raised voices they cursed and swore, stamped their feet, pounded the floor with their sticks, struck their hands, till one jumped from his seat in a rage and his gaze fell on the priest. The priest was still resting his chin on his hands, taking no more notice of them than if they were miles away. His very abstraction was a rebuke to them. The one who had jumped up said humbly, "I'm afraid we've disturbed you, Father." Captain Mellowes came to himself with a start.

"No, no, not at all," he said hurriedly. "I wasn't thinking of you at all." But the men looked as if they had offended beyond hope of pardon and kept silent till we reached the boat.

Early next morning I went up on deck. We were steaming up the river, I could see the city in the distance. Nearer to me were the famous Belfast shipyards, all alive with the clangor of hammering. As we approached I could see the swarms of men, poised on derricks and cranes, hard at work on the skeletons of ships. Just before we docked Captain Mellowes came on deck and walked over to the rail where I was standing. There was some byplay of surprised recognition between us for the benefit of those standing around. I asked him to come to the house for breakfast, and told him that he could not get a train to Dublin before ten o'clock. It was then seven o'clock and the gangplank was being put in place. I told Captain Mellowes that I was well known on the docks since the dock strike, and that it would be wiser for him to follow me instead of coming with me; that he would probably pass the Harbor Constables and policemen better alone, because, as they knew me, they would be likely to give my companion a scrutinizing glance and he would be better without that.

There were two Harbor Constables and two policemen at the end of the gangplank; they were on the watch for deserters from the Army and Navy. When I walked down the gangplank I saw that they recognized me and was glad that I had told Captain Mellowes to follow. I went in to the shed and on towards the exit. Midway I paused, dropped my suitcase as if to ease my arm, and glanced back to see if Captain Mellowes was following. He was just at the end of the gangplank; the four constables were saluting him and he was gravely saluting them.

I passed out into the street and walked slowly ahead to allow Captain Mellowes to catch up on me. In a short while we were walking together. It was too early to get a tram, and it would attract too much attention if a car drove up to our door, so we walked the distance. Falls Road, in Belfast, is called the Nationalist district, and my home was near the head of that road. When we got to that part of it where policemen were more plentiful and I was better known, I told Captain Mellowes

THE UNBROKEN TRADITION 79

to walk on ahead. I was glad I had done so, for I derived a great deal of amusement from the number of salutes Captain Mellowes had to return. Men and boys were on their way to work and they all saluted him. Every policeman on the road saluted Captain Mellowes; not one of them dreaming that the capture of the young priest they were so courteous to, would probably realize for him the dreams of Sergeantship every young policeman indulges in.

It was with a sigh of relief that I ushered Captain Mellowes into our house. The door was open and we entered without rapping. My mother thought we were the painters—she was expecting them that morning—and came out to remonstrate with us for not knocking. She was astounded for a moment, to see us in the hall, then she threw her arms around us both and literally dragged us both into the room where breakfast was on the table. She then called up the stairs to my sisters and told them we were home. On the instant there was a clatter and scamper, and pell-mell down the stairs charged my young sisters, some partially dressed and some in their nightgowns; bursting into the room they flung themselves on

Captain Mellowes, hugging and kissing him as if he were a long lost brother returned. They hung about him asking him questions, interrupting each other. They poured forth so many questions that he could not answer them much less eat his breakfast. Mother noticed that his breakfast was growing cold and turning to the youngsters said in a voice that tried to be severe, "Children. I'm surprised at you—look at your clothes." Then there was another rush to the door and a scamper on the stairs as they raced up to dress. Never were they dressed so quickly before, for in less time than it takes to tell they were down again; crowding around the table each giving the other in excitable voice the story of how Captain Mellowes managed to return; but none of them bothering to ask Captain Mellowes or myself how it really happened.

Now that Captain Mellowes was in Belfast the next thing to be done was to get him to Dublin. He could not go by train for there were detectives at all the stations. There have always been detectives at railway stations in Ireland, whose sole business is to watch and to report the arrival and departure of the important members of the Separatist Party (the revolutionary body). This method keeps the local authorities informed as to the whereabouts of "such and such a person." On this account I sought a friend who owned an automobile. It so happened that he was going to Dublin that very evening and he agreed to take Captain Mellowes with him.

When I arrived home again I saw a woman in the parlor, who looked up at me through her veil, in the most mournful way; certainly the most forlorn person I had seen in a long while. But as I went nearer I recognized the clothes. My young sisters had decked Captain Mellowes out in our clothes to see if they were skillful at disguising. They were—but the clerical clothes were better.

I told Captain Mellowes of the arrangements I had made—we were to walk into the country along the Lisburn Road for about two miles, and there meet the motor-car. When it was time we started out. We were a party of four, Captain Mellowes and another young man, who was at that time hiding from the police in our house, my sister Agna, and myself. We walked along the country road and arrived at the appointed place too soon. The car was a little late; every car that came along would lift our hearts up and when it whizzed by would leave us little more nervously excited. It came in the end, however, and stopped for a minute while Captain Mellowes was being bundled on to the car, then sped away leaving us in the dark country road.

I arrived home about one-thirty and went to bed, tired out and fully resolved to stay there for the next day. But, alas! the news had got about and after school hours some of my friends called to hear my version, and compelled me to get up. The day or so following I took part in a Volunteer play called "Ireland First" in order to give the impression that I had been in Belfast and rehearsing with the company. On Saturday my mother received a letter from my father; the only reference he made to the job he had given me was, "Tell Nora I am proud of her."

VII

AFTER that I was kept busy with the Ambulance class, and in preparing field dressings and bandages. There were about fifty girls working under my instructions and the work was beginning to be piled up. One squad was cutting up the material, another wrapping it up in waterproof material, others pasting on the directions, others sewing the completed bundle up in cotton bags which permitted them to be sewn into the men's coats. We were kept busy. When one of the officers came to the room to order the field dressings for his men, he voiced the opinion of all when he said, "Well, this looks like business. As soon as I stepped inside the door I felt that something important was going on. I suppose you all feel that way?" We did, and worked all the harder for it.

Some time before this my father had asked me if I would be in Dublin with him during the fight, but I had said, No, I would rather stay with the Northern division; that I thought I had better stay with the girls with whom I had been working. A younger sister had also decided to join the Northern detachment. My mother and the rest of the family were going to Dublin so as to be near my father. We were leaving the house just as it stood, to avoid suspicion, taking nothing from it but the trunks containing clothes. These could easily be taken without causing undue suspicion as it is quite a usual thing for families to go away for the Easter holidays. Between helping to pack up the trunks at home and the field dressings outside I managed to secure six hours' sleep during the latter part of Holy Week. My mother left Belfast on Good Friday, my sister and I the following day.

The instructions given the First Aid corps were: To meet at the Great Northern Station with full equipment and two days' rations. When we met the station was crowded with holiday-goers. There were three different queues circled around the station. We divided ourselves amongst them so that our party would not be large enough to attract attention. I found myself behind a party of soldiers going home on furlough. I could not help wondering if their furlough would be cut short, and if I might meet them again under different circumstances.

After I had taken the tickets I went to the trains to see if it were possible to get a carriage to ourselves. As the party had been split in two, one part to come on a later train, we could just fill a carriage. There was so much traffic that the railroad company had pulled out from many hiding places all the cars they could find. The line of cars presented a very curious picture as it stood waiting for the signal to start. There were the very latest corridor carriages, carriages quite new-looking, carriages old, carriages very old, and carriages so very old that they were an absolute temptation to us. These last were of that old type that has no wall between the carriages; the back of the seat is the only dividing wall. We picked out one and entered, took our seats, stowed away our haversacks, water-bottles, and hospital supplies under the seats and on the racks over our heads. Then we sat in pleasant anticipation to see who would enter the other carriage. One of the girls had put her head out of the window, and suddenly she gave a whoop and waved her arms. We hauled her in angrily, demanding to know what she meant by attracting attention in such a manner —didn't she know that the fewer that saw us the better? "But," she said when she got a chance, "I saw the Young Ireland Pipers coming up the platform looking for a carriage, and I thought it would be great to have them in the next carriage. They would pass the time for us by playing the pipes." (The Young Ireland Pipers were attached to the Volunteers.)

By this time the Pipers had come to the door of the carriage next to us and were getting in. They were both surprised and pleased when they saw the girls. They knew then that they could play all the rebel songs they desired, and say all the revolutionary things they could think of. That was one good thing about the Republican forces in our part of the country— every one knew every one else; and so it was elsewhere I am told. I doubt if ever pipers were so dressed going to battle. Slung from one shoulder was a haversack, crossing it was a bandolier filled with cartridges, a belt held the haversack in its place on one side, and from the other a bayonet was suspended. Strapped to the backs were rolled tar sheets, and under their arms they held the bagpipes with their green, white, and orange streamers flying over their shoulders. They were most warlike musicians. But more significant than all were the eager eyes shining out from under their caps. One young chap leaned over the wall and said to me, "My God! Isn't it great? We worked and worked without hope and now——" One of the boys had been tuning up the pipes and as the train began to move we swung out of the station to the tune of:

"Soldiers are we, whose lives are pledged to Ireland,
    Some have come from the land beyond the wave,
Sworn to be free, no more our ancient sireland
    Shall shelter the despot or the slave.
To-night we man the Bearna Baoighail[*]
    In Erin's cause come woe or weal,
'Mid cannon's roar or rifle's peal
    We'll chant a soldier's song."

Tyrone was our destination and we arrived there before dark. We were met by a local committee and taken to a hotel. After we had something to eat, we went over to the drill hall. There I had the first wound to attend to—one of the men had accidentally shot himself while cleaning his revolver. There was quite a crowd around me while I was dressing the wound.

[*]Barna Bail "The Gap of Danger."

88 THE UNBROKEN TRADITION

When I had finished, the men said that they hoped I would be detailed with their company, as they would feel much safer. I said that I didn't want to dress wounds till I had a chance to make some: at this they laughed and promised me that I would get all the chance I wanted. I then asked them when they would mobilize. "To-morrow morning," they replied. "We are waiting for the Belfast Division to arrive. We start on our maneuvers at 12 o'clock. We will all be together then."

We were still talking of our hopes when some one came into the hall and said that he had a message for Miss Connolly. "Here I am," I said. "What do you want?"

"Come outside, Miss Connolly," said he. "I have a message for you." I followed the man outside. The message he gave me was to the effect that the Commandant in the North had sent him to say that there would be no fighting in the North; that he had received a demobilizing order, but that he thought there would be fighting in Dublin. We could decide whether we would go back to Belfast or on to Dublin. He left the matter entirely in our own hands. I left the messenger and went back to the hall to call the girls together. I asked them to

THE UNBROKEN TRADITION 89

come with me to the hotel. I then told them the text of the message I had received and asked them to decide whether they would return to Belfast or go to Dublin. I said that I was going to Dublin and they decided to go with me. One of the girls suggested that we say the Rosary for the men who were about to fight. We knelt down and said it. We then began to get our things together again. I inquired about the trains to Dublin and was told that there would be no train till midnight. It was almost 10 o'clock then and we were some miles away from a station. I asked one of the men where I could get a car to take us to the station. They protested against our leaving, but I said that we had our work to do, and must get to Dublin as soon as possible. After some talk he sent one of the men to get two cars for us. We waited most impatiently till they came, then piling on to them as best we could we left the town and went towards the station.

While we were waiting for the train we saw the second contingent arriving from Belfast. The men had their equipment with them and swung out of the station in a truly martial way. I knew from their joyous faces and their remarks that they had not received the news we had, and I pictured to myself the change there would be when they did.

Our train left Tyrone at twelve-thirty, and arrived in Dublin at five-fifteen. We went directly to Liberty Hall for I knew my father would be there. Ever since the attempted raid on Liberty Hall, he had stayed there every night under an armed guard. He had determined that he would not be arrested before the day arrived.

As we approached to the building we saw an armed sentry keeping watch through a window; we went up the steps and knocked on the door. A sentry came to the door and asked our business. I said I was Mr. Connolly's daughter and that the girls were ambulance workers from the North. He did not know me, so he called to some one else to decide for him. The man he called to was the officer of the guard who knew me. As we went inside the door and up the stairs I asked him if he thought I could see my father. He told me that my father had not been able to go to bed until three o'clock. I said I thought it best to see my father at once. He then escorted me to the corridor in which my father's room was and told me the number. I walked along the corridor till I found the room and knocked on the door.

"Who is there?" called my father.

"Nora," I answered.

"What are you doing here? I thought you were with the North men."

"Let me in, father," I said. "I am afraid there is something wrong."

He opened the door and I entered the room. It was rather a small room, square and slightly furnished. There were but two chairs, a table, a cupboard and an army cot. My father was lying on the cot and looking at me in surprise. I went over to him and knelt down beside the cot to tell him why I was there.

"What does it mean, father? Are we not going to fight?" I asked him when I had finished.

"Not fight!" he said in amazement. "Nora, if we don't fight now, we are disgraced forever; and all we'll have left to hope and pray for will be, that an earthquake may come and swallow Ireland up."

"Then why were we told last night that there would be no fighting in the North?"

"We received word last night that there could not be got fifty men to leave Belfast."

"That is not true!" I cried. "Why, there were fifty men on the train with us leaving Belfast; and before we left Tyrone there were two hundred. I saw them myself. They are there now with all their equipment, eager and happy and boisterous with delight."

"That is a different story from what we were told," said my father.

"Mine is the true one," I returned. "But don't accept my word for it. Call in the other girls and question them."

"Ask them to come in."

I went out to the girls and said that my father would like to see them. They came in; they all knew my father but he did not know them all, so I told him all their names.

"Tell me, girls," said my father, "how many men you saw in Tyrone before you left, Belfast men particularly."

Their story was practically the same as mine. When he had heard them all, my father asked one of them to call in the guard who was on duty in the corridor. When the guard had entered the room, or rather stood at the door, my father said to him, "Call the officer of the guard."

Shortly afterwards the officer of the guard knocked on the door. I opened the door and he came inside, saluted and said, "Yes, sir?"

"Send in five men who know the city thoroughly," said my father.

"Yes, sir," said the officer as he saluted again.

"Now," said my father turning to us again. "I am going to send you to each of the other Commandants. You tell them just what you have told me. And after you tell them all, ask them to come here as quickly as they can."

The five Citizen Army men came to the room shortly after that, and each of the girls was given different addresses to go to. It fell to my lot to go to Sean MacDermott. I had as my guide a man who looked as little an Irishman as he well might be. He was short and stout yet very light on his feet; he wore bright blue overalls, short black leggings, and his face was burnt a dark brown. He wore a wide black felt hat and from under it I saw hanging from his ears, big, round gold earrings. He looked as I fancied a Neapolitan fisherman would look like.

The leaders slept no two nights in the same place. Only themselves knew where each other was sleeping. This was for safety. I was taken to a place beyond Parnell Square, about twenty minutes walk from the Hall. When we arrived there we had to knock the people up; and it was some time before we received any answer. They were very suspicious of us when I said who it was I wanted. The woman, who opened the door, consulted with some one inside the house, before she decided to let me in. The guide having done his duty in bringing me there and seeing that I was about to enter the house, went back to Liberty Hall to report.

The woman then asked me who I was, what did I want, wouldn't any one else do, and a score of other questions. She went away after she had received my answers. In a few minutes a young man came down to interview me also. I told him that I was Mr. Connolly's daughter and that Sean MacDermott knew me, and that I had a message for him from my father. He was still reluctant to let me see Sean and said that Sean had hardly had time to go to sleep. I said that I knew that but that I had been traveling all night from the

North, and had wakened my father over an hour ago who had had even less sleep than Sean.

After that he went away and came back to say that I could see Sean MacDermott. I went upstairs and found him in bed. He was looking very pale and tired. He listened to me, while I told him all I had to tell, without saying a word till I had finished. He then asked me if the others knew this. I told him that there were other girls seeing the other leaders at the same time. He remained silent for a while and then said, "I am very glad you came. Tell your father that I'll be at the Hall as soon as I can." I then returned to Liberty Hall. It was then about seven o'clock and we decided to go to Mass at Marlborough Cathedral around the corner.

VIII

When we returned from Mass my father had risen, and dressed in his uniform was going about the room singing to himself:

> "We've got another savior now,
> That savior is the sword."

I began to prepare breakfast for my father and the rest of us. But it was some time before we sat down to our breakfast, as one by one the leaders dropped into the room, and as none of them had waited to have breakfast before coming they had to be served. I remember giving breakfast to a young officer who had come up on the night mail from Limerick, for final instructions. I gave Tom Clarke his last Easter breakfast. It seemed fitting he should have as table companion Sean MacDermott—they were always such close friends. Before they had finished Joseph Plunkett, his throat heavily swathed in bandages, for he had shortly gone under an operation, arrived; and following him closely came Thomas MacDonagh. Michael Mallin and my father had their breakfast together. They were all in uniform, except Tom Clarke and Sean MacDermott. Pearse did not have his breakfast at Liberty Hall; he arrived somewhat later than the others and had already eaten. While they were all standing around and talking, one of the girls came in and said, "Mr. Connolly, look, the *Independent* says, 'No maneuvers to-day.' What does that mean? Is it a trick?"

"What is that?" said my father, taking the paper from her. "Maneuvers" was the name under which our men were being mobilized. If the *Independent,* which had the largest circulation of any Sunday paper throughout the country, printed such a bit of news it would disorganize our forces to a great extent. Yet, there it was:

Owing to the critical situation all Volunteer parades and maneuvers are canceled.
By order
Eoin MacNeill.

"What does this mean?" asked my father turning to Pearse.

"Let me see it," said Pearse. "I know nothing whatsoever about this," he said when he had read it. After that there was some low-voiced conversation among the leaders; and then the Council room. They remained there till after one o'clock.

We then ate our long delayed breakfasts and then went to another part of the Hall to see more stirring sights. On our way out of the corridor we had to pass the Council room. It was guarded by an armed sentry who stood at the door forbidding all to pass. He stopped us and would not allow us to pass until one of the officers coming out of the room saw our plight and told him who we were. When we came to the corner of the corridor we were again stopped by a sentry, but he knew me and we went on out to the front of the building.

Here, all was excitement, guards at the top and the bottom of the stairs, men and boys, women and girls running up and down; Citizen Army men arriving by the dozen armed with all their equipment, poured steadily into the great front hall.

We remained about the Hall as we had been told to stay within call in case we were needed as messengers to the North. We remained in the vicinity until well on in the afternoon. It

THE UNBROKEN TRADITION 99

was not until the Citizen Army started out on a march that we were freed. I have never been able to understand how it was that the authorities did not become aware that something untoward was afoot. There were two dozen policemen detailed to attend the Citizen Army march and they hung around Beresford Place waiting for the march to begin. Surely they should have been able to sense the difference in the feeling of the crowds that were thronged around Liberty Hall all the day. There was no disguising by the people that they expected a different ending to this march than to all the other marches. Else why the haversacks filled with food, the bandoliers filled with ammunition, and the supply wagons piled high with supplies? The men and women were under military orders. They were no longer a volunteer organization, they were a nation's army. Their fathers and mothers, their wives and children, their sisters and brothers, and their sweethearts knew that from that day forth their lives were no longer their own, but belonged to Ireland. And while they openly exulted in this thought and brought parting gifts to their loved ones, the police saw nothing.

Before they went on their march my father called me to him and told me to bring the girls to Surrey House, the home of the Countess de Markievicz, so that they would have a rest before reporting at Liberty Hall the following morning. They badly needed rest as they had had no sleep the night before. Our orders were to report at Liberty Hall the next morning at eight o'clock.

The next morning when we reached Liberty Hall we were told that we were to be given a message to take back North with us. The message was to be written and signed by Padraic Pearse; therefore we had to wait until he came. While we were waiting Thomas MacDonagh came into the room. He was in uniform. He greeted us in his gay, kindly way and pretended to jeer at us for leaving the city.

"Here we are," he said, "on the brink of a revolution and all you are thinking of is to get out of the city before we begin."

While he was talking my father came into the room carrying a large poster. He unrolled it and spread it out on the table saying, "Come here, girls, and read this carefully. It would be too dangerous to allow you to carry it with

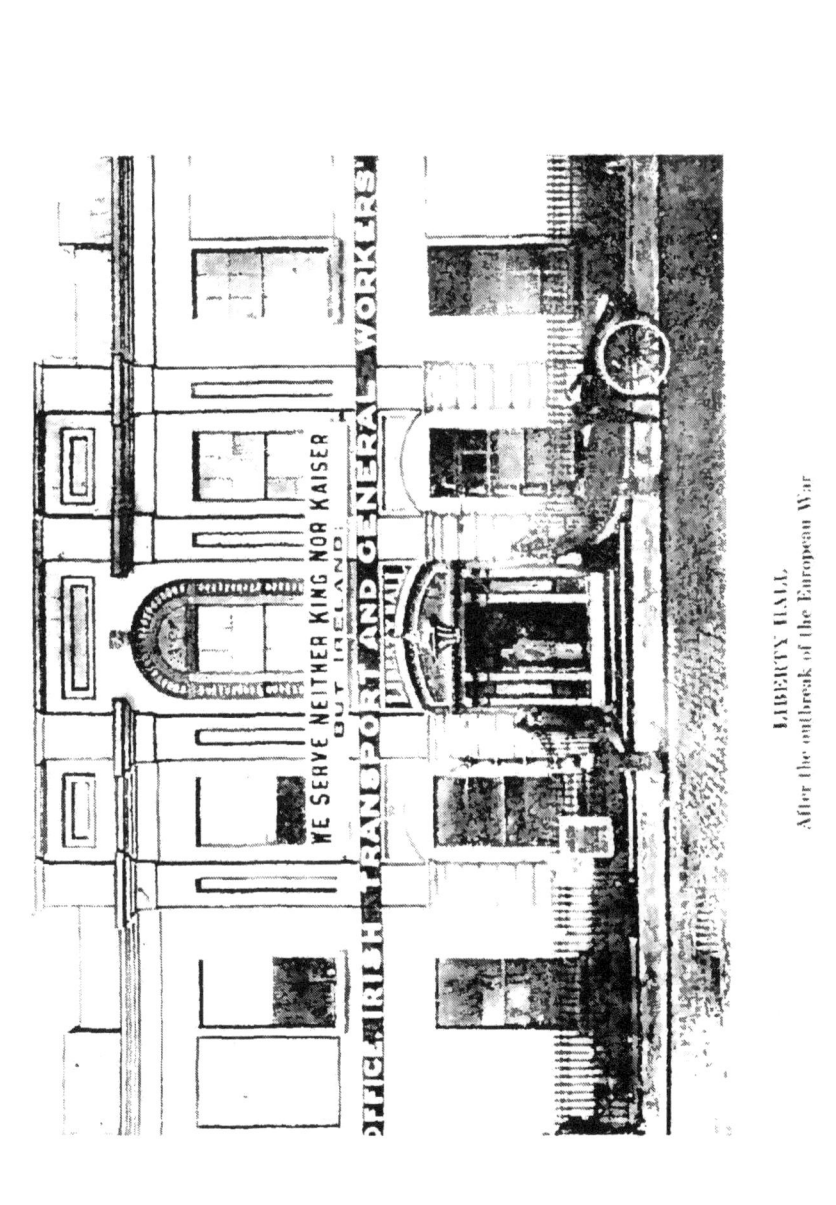

LIBERTY HALL.
After the outbreak of the European War

you, but read it carefully and tell the men in the North of what you have read." We all gathered around the table and read The Proclamation of the Irish Republic. I think that we had the honor of being amongst the first to see the proclamation.

Pearse came in while we were discussing our intended journey. He was in uniform; his military overcoat making him look taller and broader than ever. My father told him that we were waiting for the message. He went to the Council room to write it and we followed him. While we were waiting my father gave me some advice as to what we should do when we arrived in the North. Then Pearse called to us and we went to him. He handed me an envelope and said, "May God bless you all and the brave men of the North." He said it so solemnly and so earnestly that I felt as if I had been at Benediction. I then said "Good-by" to my father and left the Hall to take the nine o'clock train to the North.

IX

WE knew that the men were to rise at twelve o'clock and as that hour drew nigh we watched and listened anxiously to hear or see if the news had reached the North before us. At twelve o'clock we left the train at Portadown. There was a large body of men belonging to an Orange Band parading up and down the platform beating their drums. They were going to some meeting in Derry. The noise was terrific but we bore it gladly for it told more than words that our men in Dublin had been able to carry out their plans without any untoward accident. We changed into the other train and finished our journey in a less anxious frame of mind. But there was disappointment awaiting us at Tyrone; when we arrived there the men had already received the demobilizing order of MacNeill and had obeyed it. The Belfast contingent was already in Belfast and the country divisions had not had time to mobilize before the order from MacNeill had arrived. When I found this out I sent messengers to the various bodies advising them of what was going on in Dublin. The principal dispatch was the one given us by Pearse and that one was sent off in care of my sister, other girls going to other places. There was nothing for the rest of us to do but to await the return of the messengers.

At eight o'clock that night a boy came from Belfast who said that he had been sent to advise us to return to Belfast and asked us to go back with him. I asked the officer of the local Volunteer Corps if they intended to go on with the fight now that the men in Dublin were out, or if they intended to obey MacNeill's order. He replied that they were in honor bound to assist the Dublin men. I said that being the case I would remain with them and that we would attach ourselves to their body as they had no First Aid Corps.

About an hour later the local organizer came to the hotel and asked for me. I went out to him; he said that it would be better if we were in a less conspicuous place—would we go to some place out in the country? It was nearer to the meeting place. We agreed to go and started out about ten o'clock.

It was a night of pitch darkness, a heavy rain was pouring steadily. After a ten minutes' walk we were out on a country road where the darkness seemed to grow thicker with every step. We could see nothing but trusting to our guides soughed up and down in the mud. For twenty minutes we walked on, then we were told to turn to the right. We could see nothing that showed a turning, still we turned and found that we were in a narrower road than before. It was even muddier than the road we had left but it was shorter. At the end we were stopped by a door of what appeared to be a barn. One of the men rapped on it and it was opened to us. We stepped inside and when our eyes were used to the light again, saw a number of men with their rifles. The hall was filled with standing men, a place was cleared around the hearth upon which was blazing the biggest turf fire I had ever seen. On a bench near the fire were a half dozen women; they had brought food to the men and were now waiting to take the girls home with them. After a short wait we started out again, still following blindly where we were led. At length we came to a crossroads and there the party divided. I, along with some other girls, was taken to a large farmhouse where the folk were waiting up for us. We went into a large kitchen and sat around a big turf fire. There was porridge, in a pot hanging over the fire from a long hook, for those who liked it; and the kettle was boiling for those who preferred tea. We had a long talk around the fire. The old man told us of his experiences when he was a Fenian and drew comparisons between that time and this. Our time was nothing like his—so he told us.

In the morning we rose early; we expected to have word from Belfast every minute telling us to get on the march. But no word came that day. As the hours passed my anxiety became unbearable. I had had no word from anybody since I had come there. The men and the boys could not work for fear the word would come when they were in the fields and might be delayed if they were not on hand. And all the day long they were riding up and down the roads on the watch for the messenger who would give them the orders to rise. The second day passed, still the word never came. The men and boys came to us every hour to report all they knew. And on Wednesday at noon a man burst into the farmhouse crying,

"Pack up in the name of God, the word has come!" With what joy we packed up. How quickly the water bottles were filled and the haversacks stuffed with food. Butter, eggs, bread, and milk were thrust upon us. We could not take enough to satisfy the good people. The place was full of bustle and excitement, and then—the order was rescinded; it was a false alarm.

That disappointment ended my patience. I determined to go after my sister, who had not returned since she had left me to deliver the dispatch written by Pearse; and when we were together again we would both start for Dublin. I told the girls that I did not think that there would be any need of us in the North, that the men in command were waiting too long. That being the case it would be better for them to go home to Belfast and Agna and I would go to Dublin. They did not want to go from me, but I said I was speaking to them as their officer and they should obey. After a good deal of explaining they agreed to go home the next day.

I found that if I wanted to go to the town where my sister had gone, I would need to go by car. So a car was hired for me the next day. Just before the hour set for them to leave, a brother of one of the girls came to see what had happened to them. They all went home together. The car for myself came a little later and in it I piled as many of the Ambulance supplies as I could. There was only room for myself in the back, most of the room being taken up with the bundles. We started on our journey about six o'clock.

The town to which my sister had taken the dispatch was called Gortin; but later I had heard that she was at Carrickmore, since when I had not had any news of her. Before my mother had left Belfast she had entrusted Agna to my care, therefore I felt that I could not return without her. While on my way to Carrickmore to see if she was still there I had to pass through a village whose streets were thronged with soldiers. As we went out of the village and on into the country we met at least half a dozen motor trucks filled with soldiers. There were more marching behind, so many in fact that I asked the driver if there was a training camp near here.

"No," he said. "There is not. I'm afraid

those fellows spell trouble." Conscious that the soldiers were looking sharply at myself and the bundles, I felt more than relieved when the car spun on out of their sight.

X

It was about eight o'clock when we reached the farm at Carrickmore. Fortunately the man to whom my sister had carried the dispatch was there. As I was telling him who I was and why I had come, his sister broke on me and exclaimed sharply:

"My God! Why did you come here?"

"Why," I asked in surprise.

"Did you not meet the soldiers on your way here?" she asked.

"Indeed, I did. I saw lots of them. What are they doing here?" I asked, turning to her brother.

"They raided this place this afternoon," he said, "and have only left here three-quarters of an hour ago."

"Raided the place!" I cried. "But, of course, they found nothing."

"They did, though," he said. "They found three thousand rounds of ammunition."

"Three thousand rounds!" I cried amazed

and angry. "Where did you have it hidden?"

"In the turf stack," he replied.

"In the turf stack! Good God! What made you put it there? Doesn't every one who isn't a fool know that that would be one of the first places they would look for it. Three thousand rounds of ammunition in a turf stack! Couldn't you have hidden it some place else? Couldn't you have divided it? Couldn't you have——" and I broke off almost crying with anger and dismay.

"I know, Miss Connolly, you can't say or think anything more of the loss than I do. But I haven't been able to look after things this past week. I'm in hiding, chasing from pillar to post trying to find out what is to be done."

"And what are you going to do?" I asked. "This is Thursday and the men have been fighting in Dublin since Monday noon. What are you going to do? Think of the numbers of men and boys, women and girls who are at this minute in Dublin offering up their lives while the men of the North are doing nothing. It's a shame! It's a disgrace!"

"What could we have done? The men were all dispersed when I received the last dispatch. It's a different thing to mobilize men in the country from what it is in the city. There are a dozen or so here; six miles off there is a score; ten miles off there are some more, and so it goes all over the country. What were we to do?"

"Weren't you in a terrible hurry to obey MacNeill's order? Why were the men chased home on Sunday night and Monday morning? They were all gone when we arrived at Coalisland on Monday at one o'clock. Why were you in such a hurry to demobilize the men when their Easter holidays lasted till Tuesday? Did you not want them to fight? Were you afraid that another order would come rescinding MacNeill's?" The questions poured from me breathlessly; I was emptying my mind of all the riddles and puzzles that had been tormenting it.

"Say what you like, Miss Connolly, what can I say?" And he spread his hands in a helpless gesture.

"It's a shame," I commenced again. "Why did you not tell the men and give them the option of going on to Dublin? Why were the girls so honored? Why, the North can never lift up its head again. The men in Dublin preparing to lay down their lives while the North

112 THE UNBROKEN TRADITION

men were being chased home by their commanders. It's awful!"

"Miss Connolly, can't you believe that I feel it as much as you do? Think what it means to me that the men in Dublin are being killed while we are here doing nothing."

"The men in Dublin are fighting for Ireland. In a short while you may be fighting up here—and why? Because the Ulster Division is already quartered in Dungannon and Coalisland, and are trying to provoke a party riot by parading the streets in numbers, crying 'To Hell with the Pope.' There are bunches of them sitting on the doorsteps of Catholic houses singing 'Dolly's Brae' (the worst of all their songs). And if they go beyond bounds and those Catholics lose their temper, it will be in the power of England to say that while one part of the country was in rebellion, another part was occupied in religious fights. If you had issued another mobilization order when you received the dispatch from Pearse, that could never happen. Why didn't you issue that order?"

"We were waiting, Miss Connolly——"

"You were waiting. What for?" I broke in. "And now you have waited too long.

There has been a flying column sent from Belfast, some two hundred strong, and it has taken up such positions that you are prevented from coming together. Dungannon, Coalisland, and all around there is completely cut off from this part. There is nothing now for the North men to do but sit tight and pray to God that the Dublin men will free their country for them. My God! A manly part! Where is my sister? I want to get her and go on to Dublin. I would be ashamed to stay here while the people in Dublin are fighting."

"She took a dispatch to Clogher and is still there."

"Is Clogher far from here? Can I get there to-night?" I asked him.

"No, you cannot get there to-night; it is too far away. It is over the mountains. Stay here the night and you can set out in the morning. Stay here as long as you like, make this place your home, and don't be too hard on the North. We acted as we thought best, and perhaps we are sorry for it now. It is MacNeill's order that must be blamed. Good night, Miss Connolly."

"Are you going out? Do you not stop here?" I asked as I saw him gathering up his raincoat and cap. He straightened up his tall figure.

"No," he replied. "I have not slept here since Monday. I am determined that I shall not be arrested without doing something worth while. Good night again, and remember that this is your home for as long as you wish to stay."

"Good night," I answered as he left the room. Then it seemed that all the hopelessness of the world descended on me as I thought that here was another day gone, and I had not been able to accomplish anything.

I left the room in a few minutes and entered the kitchen. One side of the large farm kitchen was taken up by a fireplace. A large pot that was suspended over a huge turf fire the light of which reached across the room and danced and glistened upon the dishes that were standing on the top rack of the dresser. It was a sparsely furnished kitchen, for besides the dresser I could see only a table placed under the window, some farm implements on the other side of the room, and some benches. Except for the blazing of the fire there was no light, and while the ceiling was a roof of ruddy light, the rest of the kitchen was kept in semi-darkness by the farm laborers, who were sitting round the fire. The first thing I did was to arrange and make tidy my bundles of bandages which had been carried into the kitchen by the driver of the car. As I straightened up, my glance fell upon one of the men sitting by the fire, whom to my surprise I recognized as Lieutenant Hoskins of the Belfast Volunteers.

"Why, Rory," I exclaimed. "What are you doing here?"

"What are you doing here?" he asked. "I thought you were in Dublin. Didn't you go there Saturday night?"

"I did," I answered. "But I came North with a dispatch on Monday. I intend to go to Dublin to-morrow. But you didn't say what you are doing here."

"There was more chance of something happening here—we could do nothing in Belfast."

"There will be nothing happening here," I said. "That's why I am going to Dublin."

"Perhaps I'll try and make my way there to-morrow."

"I'd advise you to," I said as I left the kitchen. I was shown to my room and lost no time in getting to bed.

When my sister was leaving with the dispatch, I took her haversack from her so that she would not attract any unnecessary attention. That I might look like an ordinary traveler I put her haversack along with mine in a suitcase, and that suitcase had been carried to my room. The events of the night proved that it was a lucky thing for me that it had been brought to the bedroom. As I looked at it I wondered if a suitcase had ever before been packed in a like manner.

I could not have been asleep fifteen minutes when I was awakened by a tremendous rapping. In a few seconds the girl came to my room.

"Miss Connolly," she said. "What will we do? They are here again." I instantly thought of my revolver and cartridges which I had carried with me.

"Listen," I said. "Put on my coat and go down and open the door before they get angry."

"Why should I put on your coat?" she asked.

"Because I have something in it that I do not wish them to see. Put it on," I said, "and hurry down to the door."

When she had the coat on she went to one of the windows and opened it. She put her head out and asked who was there. While she was parleying with the soldiers I remembered that I had one hundred rounds of ammunition in one of the haversacks wrapped up in some clothing. I jumped out of bed and opened the suitcase. I had to rummage because I dare not make a light. I pulled article after article out of one of the haversacks in hot haste, but it was not there.

I turned to the other one and began searching it. I had just felt it when I heard a step on the stairs. Grasping it in my hand I sprung back into the bed. I had only arranged myself and was lying down when a light was flashed in my face.

The light was so strong that I could only lie there and blink my eyes. In a few minutes the light was removed from my face and flashed about the room, enabling me to see that it was held by a District Inspector of Police, and that he was accompanied by a military officer and some of the Royal Irish Constabulary. The D. I. switched the light back on my face suddenly and asked:

"Are you only waking up?"

"Just now," I answered.

"Don't be afraid," he said. "We heard that some more stuff came to this house to-day and we have come for it."

"It's not the most reassuring thing in the world to have soldiers and police come into your room at this time of night," I returned.

"What is your name?" he asked. I told him. I did not give a false one, as I did not know whether he had asked the girl downstairs my name or not.

"Where are you from?" was his next question.

"Belfast," I replied.

"Is that your suitcase?" he asked, pointing to it.

"Yes," I said.

"Look in it," he said to the officer.

"There is nothing there but my personal property," I said.

"All the same we must look," the D. I. said to me, as he went down to his knees beside the officer.

They gave it a rather cursory examination. Then they opened the wardrobe and looked into it, glanced into the drawers of the bureau. My heart almost stopped beating when they came near the bed. What should I do if they told me to rise? But they only looked under it, and passed out into the sitting room adjoining my bedroom. After they had examined the room they went downstairs again. I could hardly believe my luck. I was silently congratulating myself when I heard their heavy steps on the stairs again.

They came into the room again. The D. I. said, as he poured the rays of his lamp on my face, "We have found something downstairs which made us come up here to look again." I did not say anything in reply, only lay there and wondered to myself if they had found the revolver on the girl and if she had told them to whom it belonged. The military man was down on his knees at my suitcase once more.

"Did you say that there was nothing here but your personal property?" asked the D. I. as he knelt down beside him.

And then began the second search of my suitcase. Very carefully he lifted out each article and examined it. The stockings were turned inside out as a woman turns them when looking for holes. The reason for such an act I do not know, save that they might have thought that I had a dispatch concealed in them. The very fact that I knew that there was nothing incriminating in the suitcase made me lie back in the bed unconcernedly. Suddenly the officer said, "Ah!" and passed something to the District Inspector. As they were between me and the suitcase I could not see what it was. The District Inspector turned his head over his shoulder and asked again, "Did you say that there was nothing here but your own personal property?"

"I did," I replied.

"Well, what do you call this?" he asked, holding up two bundles wrapped in blue paper. "Do you call these personal property?"

"Yes, they are," I said, seeking hurriedly in my mind for an explanation. The parcel he was holding up for me to see held two dozen roller bandages. "They're mine," I said with sudden inspiration, "I got them cheap at a sale."

The answer evidently tickled the two men, for they laughed and one said to the other, "Just like a woman." They next came upon a box of tea, sugar, and milk tablets. The District Inspector asked as he held it up, "Are you going to start a commissariat department with these?"

"No," I answered. "They are no good."

Having completely overhauled my suitcase they next directed their attention to the bureau drawers. Every piece of paper in the drawers, letters, bills, etc., were read, and even the pages of books were turned over to make sure that nothing escaped them. They looked under the bed again and then passed out to the sitting room, where they remained but a few minutes. Shortly afterwards they went downstairs and then I heard them going out through the door.

Hardly were they out of the house when the girl came running to my room. "Get up, Miss Connolly," she said. "Get up and go. They'll come back and arrest you. Get up."

"Nonsense," I said. "If they intended to arrest me they would have done it now and not wait till they came back. You're excited, but there is no danger."

"You've just got to go, Miss Connolly," she said. "You can't stay here."

"That's all very well," I said. "But don't you know that I am a stranger round these parts, and if I went out now, at half past two, I'd wander away and get lost, to say nothing of the chances of my falling into the soldiers' hands. I don't intend to stay longer than the morning, in spite of your brother's invitation."

"It'll ruin this house if there is another arrested in it."

"Who has been arrested?" I asked.

"That Belfast fellow. He had his revolver, ammunition and uniform in the room with him. The policeman who arrested him said that he had enough on him to equip an army. So you see, Miss Connolly, you've got to go."

"No, I don't see," I said. "I've no intention to go out into a strange, dark country road at this hour of the night. It's no use your talking to me. I'll stay here till it's light and then I'll go, not before."

And I settled myself down in the bed. She went away, but in a few minutes her mother came to the bedside. I was hurt to the heart. I had thought of this family as patriotic. I could not understand how they could profess to love the cause, and yet wish to turn one of its workers out of the house. I could not trust myself to speak, so I turned over and showed only the back of my head to the mother and answered not a word. After a short harangue from the mother, I said, without turning my head and controlling my voice as best I could:

"I'll go when it's light."

XI

I was down in the kitchen before six o'clock. The girl had put some bread and butter on the table, a cup of tea and an egg. My heart was so full I could not eat but I managed to drink the tea. I then turned to the place where I had stacked my bundles of bandages the night before. They were gone, even the knapsack that held my few days' rations.

"Where are all my things gone to?" I asked.

"The soldiers took them away last night."

"When?" I asked. "How did they come to see them?"

"After they came down from your room the first time," she replied. "They asked me who owned those bundles. I said the girl upstairs. Then they examined them, called in the soldiers and told them to take those bundles."

"Did they take the haversack with my rations?"

"They took everything. And they asked me the name of the girl upstairs. And I said I didn't know; that you came last night and asked for a night's lodging, and that I never turned any one away from the door."

"You told them that!" I cried. "Did you want to make them suspect me? Do you usually give your guest room to women tramps? In the name of Heaven, how could you be so foolish?"

"Well," she said. "I wasn't going to let on that I knew you."

"What will I do?" I said. "Now they will be on the watch for me. I can't go to Clogher by train. I'll have to walk. How far is it?"

"It's not five miles," she answered. "You can walk it easily. About two miles from it you will come to a place called Ballygawley, and there you can get a tram that will take you to Clogher."

"Five miles," I said. "I'll get there easily before noon. Which way do I go?"

Before she answered a woman came in with a message from the girl's brother. She looked at me suspiciously till she was told who I was. I told her that I was going to walk to Clogher to get my sister who was there, and that after that we would make our way to Dublin.

"To Clogher!" she said and looked at me in astonishment.

"Yes," I said. "Does your road go near Ballygawley? If so, I'll go with you and you can point it out to me."

"Yes," she answered. "But——"

But I was already on my way to get the suitcase and did not wait to listen to her objections. As I came down again I heard the girl say:

"—that's what I'd like to know."

"Well," I said. "What I'd like to know is who the girls were who brought the message to Dublin from Tyrone. There were two, I know; one was redhaired but it was the other delivered the message by word of mouth. I'd like to know who she is."

"I brought the message," said the girl who belonged to the house.

"You brought the message," I said and stared at her. "YOU—did you know that it was a wrong one? Don't you know that you reported a false state of affairs? How could you?"

"Well enough," she answered. "You've ruined this farm with your capers. The men are unsettled, my two brothers are in hiding, and not a thing being done on the farm."

"Farm," I repeated and turned to the

visitor. I saw her blush for her acquaintance with the woman who had no soul but for a farm.

"Come," said the visitor to me. "I'll show you the road." And without another word we left. We went silently on our way. We crossed fields which brought us out on to a road, along which we walked for about ten minutes till we came to a branching of it. "We'll go up here," said my guide. I saw that it was a kind of boreen leading up to a very small farm cottage. As soon as we entered the woman turned to me and said, "We're not all like that"—not saying who or what she meant. Then again she said, "It's our shame and disgrace that our men are not helping the men in Dublin." A young man had risen from his seat when we entered. She next spoke to him and gave him a message. "It's for him," she said, nodding her head in the direction we had come from.

As she pointed to me she said to the young man, "She's going to walk to Clogher."

"To Clogher," he repeated. "It's a long walk."

"I've the day before me," I answered.

"Well, I've got my message to deliver or

I'd go part of the way with you. It wouldn't be so long or lonely if you had company."

"Thank you," I said. "But I'll get along all right."

"Can I do anything for you before you start?" asked the woman when he was gone.

"Yes," I said. "You can give me a drink of water."

"Water!" she exclaimed. "Water! Indeed you'll get no water from me! You'll just take a long drink of milk. You'll need some nourishment to bring you over the long walk that's before you." With that she handed me a huge bowl of milk. She stood by me till I finished it, then she asked me if I had anything with me to eat in case I got hungry on the way.

"No," I replied. "The D. I. and his men took away the bag containing my rations."

"Well," she said, "you've got to have something." She commenced to butter some biscuits.

"Don't bother," I said to her. "I'll get along all right without that. I'll be in Clogher about twelve."

"O, you will," she said. "Well, just take these in case you don't. And I don't think you will."

I took the biscuits, then lifted up my suitcase and started to leave the house. "Wait a minute," she cried. She went into a room and returned with a Holy Water bottle. She sprinkled me with it and said, "May God bless and look after you, and bring you safely to your journey's end."

She then pointed out the road to me and I began my walk to Clogher. The road lay between low, flat-lying lands for the better part of two miles. There was neither hedge nor ditch dividing the fields from the road; nor were there any trees for shade. It was a most lonely road; I walked on for hours and never met a soul. The sun was roasting hot that day, and I was heavily laden. Besides the suitcase containing the two kits which I was carrying, I was wearing a tweed skirt and a raincoat over my uniform. As I walked, the fields on one side of the road changed and in their place were bogs. An intolerable thirst grew upon me and there was nothing with which to slake it.

Gradually the road became a mountain road. Had I not been so tired, what with the weight of the suitcases and the clothes I was wearing and the broiling sun, I could have admired the quiet, shadeless road that stretched along for miles trimming the skirt of the mountains. The mountains sloped away so gently from the road as to seem no more than hills. Patches of olive green and brown edged with a brighter green rose one above the other, each one more pleasing. Here and there the trimming was the golden furze or whin bushes; and on towards the top patches of purple and blue told of the presence of wild hyacinths. And above all was the pure blue and white of the sky. Below, the mountains, on the left of the road stretched the bog as far as I could see, brown, brown, browner, and finally black. Here and there, standing out sharply against the dark background, danced the ceanawan—the bogrose—disputing for place with the ever-present furze. Yet all I could think of was that I must walk for miles on that lonely country road, with never a tree for shade and never a house to get a drink in.

I knew by the height of the sun that it was nearly twelve o'clock, yet I had not come to Ballygawley. In terror I thought for an instant that I had taken the wrong road, and then I remembered that the woman had told me that there was only the one road until I came to Sixmilecross.

At a distance from me and walking towards me I saw an old man. I tried to hurry towards him but could not. With every step the suitcase was growing heavier and my hands were becoming so sore that to hold the handle was absolute pain. And my thirst was growing. I could not understand how it was that I had not met with running water, it is usually so plentiful in Ireland. Finally my thirst grew so clamorous that I knelt down by the bog, lifted some of the brackish, stagnant bog-water in my hands and drank it. Immediately I began to think, "What if I contract some illness from drinking that water—what if I get fever——" And I had visions of being taken ill by the roadside with no one to look after me. But the old man was very near me now, and as we came abreast I asked him, "Am I near Ballygawley?"

"Ballygawley," he replied. "Daughter dear, you are six weary long miles from Ballygawley."

"Six miles!" I thought in despair. "How had the girl made such a mistake?"

I stumbled on till I was completely worn

out and not able to go more than a few yards at a time. And then, while I sat by the roadside feeling that I could not rise again, I saw two girls coming towards me on bicycles. When they were nearer I thought that I recognized a voice. And I was right, for one of the cyclists was my sister. I struggled up from the ditch and staggered out on to the road in dread that they might pass me. Agna jumped from her bicycle and let it fall to the ground as she saw me swaying. She helped me back to the ditch. All I could say to her at first was, "I'm thirsty, so thirsty." She peeled an orange and gave it to me. I knew that I was babbling all the time, but neither of us could remember what I had been saying when we tried to think of it afterwards. I did not know that I had been crying till Agna said, "Don't cry, Nora. Here, let me wipe your eyes." Then I saw where the tears had splashed down on my raincoat and felt that my cheeks were wet. I suppose I was weeping from sheer physical exhaustion.

"Weren't we lucky to come this road, Teasie? This is my sister Nora," said my sister to the girl who accompanied her. "We were going to take the lower road," she said,

132 THE UNBROKEN TRADITION

turning to me, "but we were told that although this was the longer it was the easier for cycling. And now, I'm glad we took the longer one, for if we hadn't we would never have met you."

"Where were you going?" I asked.

She told me.

"Why," I cried, "that is the place I have left."

"Is that so?" said Agna. "Then we needn't go. You can tell us the news. We wanted to find out what happened during the raid yesterday."

As I sat there on the ditch I told them all that had happened from the capture of the three thousand rounds of ammunition to my own experiences. When I finished Agna took the suitcase and balanced it on her bicycle and said:

"We may as well go back now."

"I'll cycle on in to Ballygawley," said Teasie, "and find out when there will be a train this afternoon. You can come on after me."

"How far are we from Ballygawley?" I asked.

"About two miles," she answered.

"Never mind," said Agna, when she saw my

expression at that news. "We will go so slowly that you'll never notice it."

The three of us went slowly along the road, Agna and Teasie taking turns at carrying the suitcase. At a turn in the road Teasie mounted her bicycle and rode off. After we had walked a long distance I said:

"Agna, I can't walk any further. I'll have to sit down."

I sat for quite a while till Agna said, "Try again, Nora. Keep at it as long as you can. When we get to Ballygawley you'll not have any more walking to do."

"Wait a while," I answered.

While we were sitting Teasie returned.

"You'll be in plenty of time," she said.

I stood up and we started off again. When we arrived at the outskirts of Ballygawley Teasie said, "I called in at a house I knew and they are making tea for us. You'll be refreshed after it."

It was into a shop we went and in a room back of it a table was laid, and tea was ready for us. I drank the tea thirstily but was too tired to eat, although various things were pressed on me. When tea was over Teasie said to Agna:

"We'll go on our bicycles and meet Nora at the station of Augher. That," she said, turning to me, "is the station before Clogher. I think it would be better to get off there than in the station at Clogher. Every one would see you and they would be making all the guesses in the world as to who you are. The police would see you, too, as you would have to go past the police station. If you get off at Augher you can cross the fields to our place without any one seeing you. That's all right, isn't it?"

"Yes," I said.

They rode away. A young lad took my suitcase to the station for me and waited till the train came. The train was only the size of a trolley but had the dignified title of the Clogher Valley Railway. I sat in the corner and closed my eyes. I opened them at every stop to see if there was any sight of the girls. But it was not till the conductor called out, "Next stop Augher," that I had any glimpse of them. Over the hedge that divided the rails from the road I saw Agna's black curly head bobbing up and down and caught a smile from under Teasie's big-brimmed hat. They were peddling for all they were worth in an attempt not to be too far behind the train in arriving at Augher.

I waited at the station for about ten minutes before they came. They jumped off their bicycles; and we commenced to walk along the side of the rails. About fifteen minutes after we crossed over into a field. It was a stiff piece of work for the girls to push their bicycles through the fields and lift them over hedges. When we had gone through four fields we commenced to climb a hill. Near the top of the hill we clambered over another hedge and crossed one more field before we arrived at the farm which was Teasie's home. Teasie's father and mother had made it a home for Agna since she arrived at the town; and to me they also extended a very kindly welcome.

"She has walked all the way from Carrickmore," said Teasie to her mother. "We met her two miles outside of Ballygawley."

"Did you walk all that distance?" asked Mrs. Walsh.

"Yes," I answered. "I don't see how it took me so long to walk it, I'm usually a good walker."

"When did you start?" she asked me.

"Before eight," I answered.

"I think you did very well to walk it in one day," she returned. "Agna and Teasie were going to cycle there and stay over night because it was such a long ride."

"I was told that it wasn't five miles," I said.

"Five miles!" cried the mother. "It's fifteen if it's one, and a bad road at that. You'll want to rest after it. Take her into a bedroom, girls, and let her lie down."

The girls brought me to a bedroom and gave me cool water to bathe my face and hands and feet. Then they ordered me to go to bed. But although I went to bed I did not sleep.

I had been lying there for about two hours when Agna peeped in to see if I was awake.

"Come in," I said.

"Nora, what are we going to do?" was her first question.

"I am going to Dublin as soon as we can and you, of course, are going with me."

"I had my mind made up to try and get there to-morrow when we came back, but I am glad you are here, for now we can be together and won't have to worry about one another." She was speaking in her usual breathless fashion. "I'm afraid we can't go

THE UNBROKEN TRADITION 137

to-night," she said. "Did you hear that there is fighting in Ardee?"

"No," I answered. "I did not hear that; but if there is, we'll go there. It's on our way to Dublin. The men who are fighting will probably make their way to Dublin. If we can catch up with them we will be safer and more sure of getting there. Find out if there is a train to-night."

She went out and returned in a few minutes.

"No," she said. "There is no train to-night, but there is one leaving at five minutes to six in the morning."

"Well," I said. "I suppose we'll have to wait for that."

We caught the five minutes to six train in the morning. It brought us to a junction where we took tickets for Dundalk.

"You're going to a dangerous place," said the ticket agent.

"We won't mind that," we replied.

When we arrived at Dundalk the station was full of soldiers and constabulary. We hurried along out of the station so as not to attract attention. Agna went back and asked a porter if she could get a train to Dublin. The porter told her that the only train going there was a military one, and that the line was in the hands of the military. "There's no telling when there will be a train," he said.

It was then about one o'clock. "Come along," I said to Agna. "We will look for a restaurant and decide what we will do while we are eating." We walked down the street looking for a restaurant. At the foot of the street we saw one, a very small place. Just at the restaurant the street curved, and around the curve we saw that a barricade had been erected by the police authorities. Luckily we did not have to pass it to get to the restaurant. When we had entered and had given our order to the proprietress, she said that it would take some time—would we mind waiting? We assured her that we would not mind waiting and went into the parlor to talk over our situation.

The first decision arrived at was, that as we did not know the name of the villages and towns on the road to Dublin and could not hire a car to take us to any of them, it would be necessary for us to walk. Our next decision was that we would have to abandon our suitcase as it would be likely to attract attention. In order to carry out the second I told Agna that she must go out to buy some brown paper

THE UNBROKEN TRADITION

and string. Also, that while she was doing so she must find out if we would have to pass the barricade to get to the Dublin road. The reason why I sent Agna on this business, and did not go myself, was that Agna was so childish looking that no one would suspect her of trying to get to Dublin. Then again I knew that I could trust her to find any information necessary to us; she had been a girl scout and had learned the habit of observation. Also, her accent was more strongly Northern than mine.

With a parting adjuration from me not to be too long lest I become anxious, Agna went out on her errand. As she reached the door the proprietress came out of a room and said, "Are you going out, little girl?"

"Yes," said Agna. "I am going out to get a paper."

"Will you do a message for me while you are out?"

"Certainly," said Agna. "What is it?"

"Do you know the town?" asked the woman.

"No," said Agna. "I haven't been in it this long time." (She had never been in it before.)

"Well," said the woman. "I had better

come to the door and show you the place I want you to go to." She did so and gave Agna a message to the butcher's. Agna was glad to do the message because if she were stopped now and asked where she was going to, she could give a definite answer. She left the door and walked towards the barricade. The policeman on duty there did not stop her as she walked through. The barricade was formed simply of country carts drawn across the roadway, leaving room for only one vehicle to pass through, and it was at this space that the policeman stood. As I sat by the window, I saw the policeman stop and examine cyclists, automobilists, and all other vehicles that were passing through. The barricade was on the road running from Dublin to Belfast.

Within twenty minutes Agna returned. She came into the parlor and gave me a bundle of brown paper and string, and then went out to deliver up her other message. She came back quickly and began to tell me the result of her observations. The best thing was that we were on the right side of the barricade and we should not have to pass it when we started out. But her next bit of information was not so pleasant; it was that according to the automobile signs there were fifty-six miles to Dublin. Still, nothing daunted, we began to transfer our kits from the suitcase to the brown paper. When we had finished we had two tidy-looking bundles much more convenient to carry than the suitcase.

While we were eating our dinner the question arose as to what we should do with the suitcase. We settled it by asking the proprietress to take care of it till we came back from Carlingford. She was quite willing to oblige us, she said, as Agna had been so obliging to her. I then paid the bill and we left the restaurant. I felt rather badly at leaving the suitcase behind me, as it had accompanied me for some ten thousand miles of my travels; it was like abandoning an old friend.

XII

It was about two-thirty on Saturday when we started to walk from Dundalk to Dublin, and when it began to grow dark we were still walking. While we were discussing the problem of where to spend the night, we came upon a barricade. We were in a quandary. What were we to do? We slowed up in our walking but that was no use; we were bound to pass it eventually—or be detained. We had not the slightest idea as to what we should do. We did not know the name of the next village, so we could not say that we were going there. We did not even know the name of the village we were in! What should we do? If we were stopped and searched—I had my revolver and ammunition and Agna wore her uniform under her coat and skirt—enough evidence to have us arrested. However, we put on a brave face and stepped forward bravely towards the barricade. About six yards from it we encountered two strong wires which were stretched across the entire width of the road, one reaching to the chin and the other to the knees. To give the impression that we had passed that way before and that we knew all about the wires, we ducked our heads under the high wire and put our legs over the lower one, then continued our walk to the barricade.

It was in charge of a corporal's guard. As we came abreast the soldiers, evidently thinking that we were country girls doing our Saturday's marketing, made some remark, in a broad Belfast accent, about carrying our bundles for us. In an accent broader than theirs, Agna gave them some flippant answer at which they roared with laughter; and while they were laughing we passed on. Further on we came to the village proper. Not until we saw the sign over the Post Office—"Dunleer P. O."—did we know the name of the village through which we were passing.

As we walked it grew darker. "What will we do—where will we spend the night?" I said to Agna. "There are no hotels about here, and if there were we could not go to them as we would have to register. If we ask at the cottages for a night's lodging they may become suspicious. If we walk all night we may meet military or police patrols, and that would mean that we would be sent to Armagh Jail instead of going to Dublin. What will we do?"

"O, pick out a nice field and spend the night there," said Agna airily.

"It looks as if that is just what we'll have to do," I said ruefully. "Come on and pick one before it gets too dark."

We heard a dog barking further down the road—that was the only sign of life. We judged that it was about nine o'clock and that every one was in bed. There was a path that turned to the right off the road which we took and walked along for about one hundred yards. Then we clambered over the hedge and into the field. It looked as if we had chosen a good place for we found ourselves in a sort of dell covered with grass and heather. We searched and found, as we thought, the softest place. Everything around us was so still that we felt compelled to talk in whispers. We could feel the darkness descending on us as we sat there, forgetting our weariness in the novelty of the situation.

THE UNBROKEN TRADITION 145

We had been silent for a long time when Agna said, "To-morrow will be Sunday."

"Yes," I said. "We'll look queer carrying bundles through the villages on a Sunday."

"So we will," said Agna. "Look," she said suddenly. "Why couldn't we put on everything we can. It will make us fatter but it will make the bundles a respectable size. And we'll be warmer to-night," she added.

Her last remark decided me. I had been growing colder every minute I sat there and any suggestion to relieve me was welcome.

"All right," I said. "Let's start and put them on."

We opened the bundles and were very busy for some time. When we had finished there was twice the amount of clothing on than we had when we begun. We looked at each other, feeling bulky.

"I hope my coat will go on me," said Agna as she began to put it on. "There now, I've got everything on me except my towels, and brush and comb. Oh, and my putties."

"You can put them in your coat pocket," I said.

"I've got safety pins, roller bandages, my

handkerchiefs and my purse in them so there's no room there."

"Put them in your raincoat pocket." She did so and stood up to inspect herself.

"O Lordy," she exclaimed. "I'm an imitation umbrella." Then she turned her attention to me.

"How did you get on?" she asked.

"Like you," I replied. "Only I've a pair of stockings left."

"Put them on you?" she said. "What's the use of getting boots two sizes too big for you, if you can't wear two pairs of stockings when you want to?"

I had forgotten that I could not get my size when I was buying my marching boots, and was compelled to take a pair two sizes too large. I put the stockings on.

"I never felt so big and heavy in my life before," I remarked.

"You'll be used to it by morning," she said consolingly. "Lie down and go to sleep."

"Sleep—" I commenced when she interrupted me to ask, "Nora, do you think there are any earwigs here? They might get into our ears when we are asleep."

"Earwigs," I repeated. "I don't know.

But there's bound to be other insects and they would just as easily get into our ears as earwigs."

"What will we do?" she asked anxiously, for she was tired and wanted to sleep. I looked about and saw the towels.

"Put them around our heads," I said, pointing to them. So we each took a towel and pinned it around our heads to keep out wandering insects while we slept. But we need not have worried about what might happen to us while we slept, for we did not sleep that night.

As we lay there we could see the stars come out one by one, yet we could not sleep. The quietness of the place kept us listening expectantly for we knew not what. A heavy mist began to cover the field and wrapped itself about us till our clothes were dampened through and through. For the first time, I think, we were physically aware of the number of bones in our bodies, for each one seemed to be dancing to a tune of its own. Our teeth were chattering so that we could not speak. In an effort to keep ourselves warm we lay close together with our arms round each other. But our efforts were of no use; we could not sleep nor could we keep ourselves warm. We gave the struggle up and huddling close to the ditch we sat and waited for the dawn.

After an infinity of time the dawn came. Far off at the furthermost edge of the field we saw a streak of gray. As we watched it gradually widening we heard a cock crow in the distance. Under the descending light the fields seemed a glistening sea and our tweed skirts as if sprinkled with diamonds. The birds began to awaken and to chirrup in the hedges. For all we could see or hear, the birds and ourselves were the only stirring, living beings.

We sat on waiting for time to pass. As we did not have a watch with us we gauged the time by the sky. The distance between us and Drogheda we knew to be less than eight miles; and there was a possibility that we might get a train from Drogheda to some of the local stations. But as we were not sure we decided to recommence our walk, so that we would be all the earlier on our way to Dublin. With this thought in our minds we rose stiffly and plodded down the path to the main road. We really did not feel tired. As a matter of fact, we were anxious to have as many adventures and experiences as possible to tell our father when we reached Dublin. We pictured ourselves sitting on his knees, as we had often done before, telling him everything, watching for the ever-ready twinkle in his eye, and saw him give the quick throwback of his head, when we came to the more laughable parts of our story. It was this picture that helped us over the hard parts of our journey. As we went along the road to Drogheda our conversation consisted mainly of—"Wait till we tell Papa this—" or, "What will Papa say to that—" and, "Won't he laugh when we tell him—," so we whiled away the time, fixing firmly in our minds the most amusing parts of our journey.

It was not until we were within two miles of Drogheda that we met with any one on the road. The first person we saw was a cyclist, next we saw a man and woman going to milk the cows. And then as we went further along the road we saw many more people wending their way to town. At last, we came to Drogheda. It was practically deserted—a few milk-carts and a couple of policemen were all that we met as we proceeded into town. Then a church bell began to ring. We followed the sound and soon had joined a crowd that was hurrying to church. We were in time for seven o'clock Mass.

After Mass we wandered about a little hoping to find a place where we could get something to eat, also to find the road to Dublin. On account of it being Sunday and so early in the morning there was no place open. Although hungry we were not as much annoyed at the result of our search for food as contented when we came upon the road to Dublin. As we walked on I saw the railway station. A thought struck me, perhaps we can get a train now. I turned to Agna and said, "Go up to the station and ask if there will be a train to Skerries to-day."

In about fifteen minutes she returned and said there would be no trains running but the military trains. Then once again we started on our tramp.

Agna complanied of hunger, and I was none the less hungry. We had not eaten since one-thirty the day before. "Would it be any use, do you think," I asked, turning to Agna, "to call at some of the cottages and ask them to make some tea for us?"

"It might be worth trying, anyway," she replied.

"Well," I said. "I'll wait till it gets a little later then I'll go to some of the cottages and ask."

It was after nine o'clock when I first ventured to a cottage. A woman opened the door to my knock, she had a bonnet on and was draping a shawl about her shoulders.

"We have been walking since early morning," I said, "and want to know if you will make us a cup of tea."

"I would," she replied, "only I've barely time to get to Mass. I'm sorry, but I can't miss Mass. I've to walk to Drogheda."

"No," I said. "It wouldn't do to miss Mass."

She came to the gate and bade me a cordial good-by. I tried two or three cottages after that, but from them all I had the same story—they were all going to Mass, so we had to go without our breakfast.

Just outside Drogheda we saw a milestone bearing the legend "Dublin 25 miles." And from then on the only excitement of our journey was to see who would be the first to spy a milestone. When we saw a milestone marked "Dublin 18 miles" we were exhilarated —Dublin seemed only a few steps away.

Sunday was, if any thing, warmer than the preceding day, and our double outfit made us dreadfully uncomfortable. I knew that it was not the heat or the long walk, or the two pairs of stockings that was responsible for the burning pain in my feet. My feet were burning me as never before. Agna had great faith in liniment. She likes to take it with her when she goes for a long walk; she says it takes the pain and stiffness from her muscles. When we were making our preparations the night before she had "linimented" herself as she calls the operation. I had had no pain or tiredness, but the soles of my feet were sore, and Agna, in her unfailing faith in the bottle, had "linimented" them, overruling whatever objections I had. And now, I was suffering torments—the liniment was burning its way into my flesh, made tender by the two pairs of stockings, heavy boots, and long march. At last, I could stand it no longer, so I said to Agna, "I must get my boots and stockings off—I'll have to get some relief or I'll go mad."

I walked towards the hedge that was dividing the road from the fields and looked through the branches. I saw that the land was

EOIN MACNEILL
Professor of Early Irish History, Head of the Irish Volunteers, whose demobilization order "broke the back of the rebellion," according to the report of the British Royal Commission Yet in spite of this he was sentenced to prison for life.

THE UNBROKEN TRADITION 153

plowed. It looked so cool and comforting that I decided to go in to cool my feet. We walked along till we saw a gap in the hedge. We went through it and found ourselves in a shady corner of the field. I lost no time in pulling off my shoes and stockings, and then I thrust my feet deep down in the cool, brown earth.

How long we sat there I do not know for we both dozed off. Then we heard a distant dull booming which must have awakened us. Agna must have wakened at the same time as myself for she was listening, her head turned away from me, and her ear cocked in the direction from which the booming came. The booming went on at regular intervals. At last, Agna turned to me, her eyes widened and a thought written on her face that she did not dare to express in words.

"What is it, Nora?" she asked.

I shook my head. "It's in Dublin," I answered.

"There might be fighting in the Irish Sea," she hazarded.

"No, it's in Dublin," I insisted. We were silent for a while, a great dread growing in our hearts. Agna broke the silence.

"Dublin, Nora," she said. "And we are—"

"We are eighteen miles away from Dublin," I said.

When we had seen the last milestone that told us that we were eighteen miles away from Dublin, we thought we were very near; but now, our thought was how very far away we were from there.

The booming continued. We could picture our friends, our comrades, boys and girls fighting with rifles against those big guns whose booming could be heard eighteen miles away.

"We must not lose a minute. We must hurry, hurry, hurry till we get to Dublin," I said, and saw that unconsciously I had been putting on my shoes and stockings, and that I was ready for the march.

In the torment of our minds as to what those big guns might be doing at the moment in Dublin, the pain, the weariness and the hunger of our bodies went unnoticed. We swung along as best we could, trying to keep to the beat of a march, and determined to be in Dublin before dark. We entered a village. Usually when we came to a village we walked at an ordinary pace so as not to attract notice by an appearance of haste. But this time, in our impatience to be in Dublin, we threw all cautiousness to the winds and went as quickly as we could. We passed through the village; but just as the main street ended and the Dublin road began again, we saw a barricade. Like the others it was made of country carts, but unlike them it was guarded by both police and soldiers. They seemed to be more particular at this one for we saw them stop a cyclist and give his bicycle a most thorough examination. They looked under the saddle, and into the tool-bag; and then they turned their attention to the rider. His pockets were turned out one by one. I suppose they were looking to see if he carried a dispatch.

After him came two boys who were stopped as they were walking past. We were almost at the barricade by this time and we saw close beside it a restaurant. As usual they had left a space for pedestrians to pass through and unfortunately for us, the door of the restaurant was on the other side of the barricade. It was, if I might use the phrase, next door to it. But the boys, who had just been stopped by the military, unintentionally did us a good turn, for they began to resist being searched.

156 THE UNBROKEN TRADITION

While they were talking indignantly, and struggling with the soldiers, Agna and I slipped through into the restaurant. When we had asked for something to eat we went to the window to see what was the outcome of the struggle. To our surprise, we saw the boys laughing and chatting with the soldiers who were examining their pockets.

We did not realize how hungry we were till we began to eat our dinner. We finished all before us for we had not eaten since lunch the day before; and it was three o'clock then. The waitress kept hovering around as if she would like to speak, but did not know how to begin. At length she asked us if we were going far.

"To Clontarf," I answered.

"O," she said disappointedly. "I thought you might be coming from Dublin, and would have some news."

"No," I said. "We haven't any; we left Drogheda this morning and there was no news there."

"Did you hear how things were going in Dublin?" she asked.

"No," I answered. "Did you?"

"Well," she said. "I heard they were sur-

THE UNBROKEN TRADITION 157

rendering in Dublin—that they were beaten. But I don't believe it," she added quickly.

"Nor do I," I said. "They couldn't be beaten so soon."

"That's what I've said all along," she said. Evidently she was a rebel and was trying to find out if we were, too. But before we could carry on any further conversation we heard the soldiers call "Halt," and then we saw a motor car stopping outside the window.

The waitress put her head out the window and began to chaff the occupants of the car.

"Are you bringing ammunition to the Sinn Feiners?" she asked them.

"How many Sinn Feiners have you hidden in the car?"—and so forth.

While she was doing this I said to Agna, "Come, we'll look out, too, then the soldiers may think we belong here." We did so and also joined in the chaffing while the soldiers were searching the car. When they had allowed the car to go on the waitress said to them in a very sarcastic tone:

"All day at it and you haven't caught a single Sinn Feiner yet?" The soldiers looked up at us and grinned sheepishly; but they did not seem the least disturbed at their failure to catch one.

We turned in from the window, paid our score, and went out of the restaurant just as the sergeant in command of the barricade was stepping in. My heart gave a great leap. "Was he coming in to question us?" I asked myself. But he made way for us and we went out into the street. This time we were on the right side of the barricade; still there was a chance of our being stopped. However, we looked at the soldiers, nodded and smiled to them, received nods and smiles in return and walked down the Dublin Road.

Balbriggan was the name of the town we had just left, some fifteen miles from Dublin. Now that we were refreshed by the meal, Dublin seemed no distance away from us, and we felt sure that we could reach it before dark. We met more people on this road than we had met within all the rest of our journey, some going towards Dublin, some towards Drogheda. Many a bit of news we heard as it was called across the road by friends as they passed. But there was none that we could rely upon as each bit contradicted the other.

THE UNBROKEN TRADITION 159

Still we began to feel that there was bad news in store for us.

We had gone along the road for about four miles when I suddenly became lame; the big muscle in my right leg was powerless. I kept on as best I could dragging my right leg after me. When I had gone about a mile this way I grew desperate. The pain was almost more than I could bear, and the milestones were dreadfully far apart. Then I said to Agna, "The first car that comes along I'll ask for a lift."

The first car that came along was a big gray touring car occupied by a lady and gentleman. I did not ask them for a lift; but the gentleman looked back at us after he had passed.

"Perhaps he knows us," said Agna. "It might be some of our friends dispatching."

"No, he's not," I answered.

"Well, he's stopping," returned Agna. "Hurry up. Perhaps he will give us a lift."

"I can't hurry," I said. "I'm going as best I can."

"Look," said Agna. "He's backing up towards us."

160 THE UNBROKEN TRADITION

She was right. The big car was backing up to us. When it was near the man asked,

"Are you going far?"

"To Clontarf," answered Agna.

"I'm going within six miles of it. If you care to get in I'll take you that length."

"Thank you very much," said Agna. "My sister is almost done up."

"You're from the North, aren't you?" asked the man when we had taken our seats in the car.

"Yes," I answered. "We left Drogheda this morning."

"Who are you going to in Clontarf?" he asked after he had driven for some distance.

"My mother," I said. "She came down for the Easter holidays and has not been able to get away. She's probably terrified out of her senses as she has the two youngest children with her."

"She's probably hungry, too," he said. "Did you bring her food?"

"No," I said. "But we brought her money."

"Food would have been better," he said. "People who live on the outskirts of Dublin are in a bad way. They've always depended on Dublin for their supplies. They can get none now. I've just been to Drogheda for bread."

"To Drogheda for bread," I repeated in amazement.

"Yes," he said. "It's no joke to have to go twenty-five miles for bread. Weren't you two girls afraid to come down here?"

"We had to come," I said simply. "Papa couldn't come so he sent us."

All this time we had been spinning along at a splendid rate. We were cooled off and feeling rested. Suddenly the man slowed up the machine. "Hello, what's this?" he said. We followed his gaze and saw that the telegraph wires had been completely cut through; not one wire was left together. "Hm," he said. "We must make a note of that and keep our eyes open for more." There was no more conversation after that for some time. On our way we saw the wires cut in two places.

After some time we came to a village. There was a guard of soldiers patrolling the street in front of a building. When we came nearer we saw that it was the police barracks; and that the windows were broken and the street strewn with telegraph wires.

"O?" I said, wondering what it could mean.

"Yes," said the man. "The rebels came here, captured the police barracks, took every rifle and all the ammunition, and marched away to Dublin or Wexford. But before they did that they cut down all the telegraph wires and stopped all communication between this town and any other. They made a good job of it—every man of them got away."

He then left the car to go over to speak to the soldier in charge. When he returned he said, "I told him about the wires being cut further up the road. And then we started off again. He stopped the car outside of the village near a bridge and told us that he was not going any further. We stepped out of the car and thanked him for his kindness in bringing us so far.

"Not at all," he said. "Don't mention it. Glad to help any one."

We watched him as he turned the car up a driveway of an estate near the bridge; wondering if he would be glad to think that he had helped the daughters of the Commandant-General of the Rebels to reach Dublin.

XIII

WE had been walking only half an hour when we saw a cavalry regiment coming towards us and leaving Dublin. First came the advance guard, then a long line of soldiers and horses, and then their artillery and their supply wagons, and more soldiers brought up the rear. They made a brave show tearing along the country road raising a dust as high as the horses.

"Nora, Nora," wailed Agna. "They're leaving Dublin—they're leaving it—not going to it. Our men must be beaten."

"Hush," I said to her. "They may be going to some place else."

I stopped an old man and asked him, "Where are they going? I thought the fighting was in Dublin."

"They're going to Wexford," he replied. "The rebels have captured two or three towns and are holding them. These fellows," pointing with his thumb over his shoulder at the soldiers, "are going down to try and drive them out. God curse them," he added, spitting towards the soldiers.

"There now," I said as I turned to Agna. "Isn't that good news? Wexford out and the West awake! East and West the men are fighting for Ireland. For Ireland, Agna! O, aren't you glad to be alive! We used to read about the men who fought for Ireland and dream about them, and now, in a couple of hours we'll be amongst the men and women who are fighting in Dublin. We'll be able to do something for Ireland."

That thought cheered us so and spurred us on that we arrived in Drumcondra, a suburb of Dublin, at seven o'clock on Sunday night.

We were going to the house of a friend in Clonliffe Road. On our way there we were astonished at the ordinary aspect of the streets. Save for the fact that we saw no soldiers, we could have thought that there had been no fighting at all. Dublin is the most heavily garrisoned city in Europe. Ordinarily one could not walk the streets without seeing scores upon scores of soldiers. Therefore, our not seeing them was a sure sign that things were not in Dublin as they had been. When we

MAP OF DUBLIN

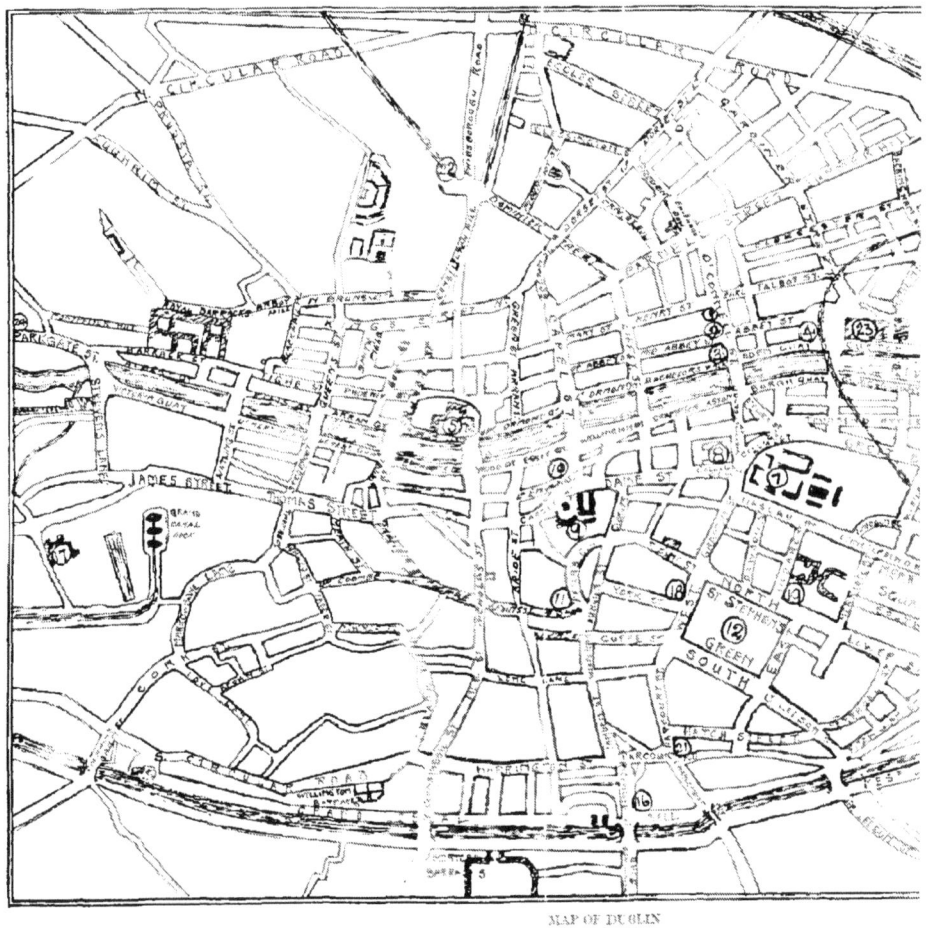

reached the house of our friend, the two daughters, Kathleen and Margaret, were at the door.

"My God!" said Margaret, when she spied us.

"Where have you come from?" asked Kathleen, looking at our travel-worn figures. Our faces were burnt red by the sun and the heat, and our boots were white with the dust of the road.

"We've come from Tyrone. We got a train to Dundalk and walked the rest. We spent last night in a field. What's the news? How are things down here?" I asked.

"How are things," she repeated in amazement. "Haven't you heard?"

"Nothing," I answered, as I shook my head.

"The boys are beaten," she cried. "They've all surrendered. They're all prisoners. The city has been burning since Thursday."

"All surrendered," I cried aghast. "Are you sure? It doesn't seem possible."

"Yes," she said. "I'm sure. They're all prisoners, every one of them. The College of Surgeons was the last to surrender and it surrendered a little while ago. Madame was there," she said, meaning the Countess Markievicz.

I sat there too stunned to think or talk. I knew that there were women and men going past the window, yet I could not see them. After a while I managed to ask, "My father?"

"He's wounded and was taken a prisoner to Dublin Castle. They don't think he'll live. Though God knows maybe they'll all be killed."

I was roused from a dazed condition by the sharp crack-crack-crack of a rifle.

"What does that mean?" I asked, turning to Kathleen.

"My God!" she exclaimed. "Are they starting again?" But there was no further reports.

"Can I get across the city?" I asked.

"No," she answered. "We are not allowed out of our own district. And anyway we must not be out after seven; martial law has been declared."

"Must not be out after seven," I repeated. "But it's after seven now, and there are lots of people out there on the street."

"They're at their own doors," she said indignantly. "We can stay around our own doors, I hope. Though," she added, "if the soldiers order us to go inside we must obey."

"I wanted to get to Mamma," I said. "She'll be in a dreadful state."

"Where is she now?" asked Margaret.

"At Madame's cottage in Dundrum," I answered.

"There's no way of getting there," she said. "There's neither trains nor trams running now."

"We can walk," I said. "It's only six miles and we are well used to walking by now."

"Well," said Kathleen. "There's no use talking about it now. You can't go and that's all there is to it. The best thing you can do is to eat something and then go to bed. In the morning we can see what is to be done."

I agreed with that as we sorely needed the rest; but it was a sorry ending to all our hopes and expectations. On our way down we had been buoyed up by the thought that at last we would be able to do something for Ireland. Something, anything that would help on the fight. That our men would still be fighting we never doubted. And now the fighting had stopped before we came. We could never sit on my father's knee and tell the tales of our adventures. He was a prisoner, and wounded, and like to die. Perhaps we would never see

168 THE UNBROKEN TRADITION

him again; perhaps Mamma would never see him again. Were the men really beaten? Sharp pain-swollen thoughts came thronging through my head as I lay on my bed listening to the sharp crack of a rifle where some lone sniper was still keeping up the fight.

Early in the morning Kathleen came into our room.

"What do you think?" she exclaimed excitedly. "They're building a barricade at the top of this street."

"They must expect the fighting to be resumed," I said.

We dressed hurriedly and went down to the drawing room. From the window I saw the soldiers entering the houses at the top of the street, and taking furniture from them with which to build a barricade. It stretched clear across the street, leaving a space open on the left side. At that space a guard of soldiers were stationed. Kathleen went down to the barricade to ask for permits which would allow us to pass it and through the city. She was refused the permits. But we were not discouraged at the failure of our first attempt. Kathleen, Agna and I went in another direction till we met the sentries at the bridge on

THE UNBROKEN TRADITION

Jones' Road. Here we were allowed to pass and after a circuitous route we arrived at the top of O'Connell Street, near the Parnell statue.

There were evidences of the fighting all around us. We saw the buildings falling, crumbling bit by bit, smoldering and smoking; a ruin looking like a gigantic cross swayed and swayed, yet never fell. I was reminded of pictures I had seen of the War Zone. Here were the same fantastic remains of houses. Crowds of silent people walked up and down the street in front of the Post Office. The horrible smell of burning filled the air. And on one side of the street were dead horses.

We saw the General Post Office, the headquarters of the rebels, still standing, although entirely gutted by fire. The British gunners in their attempt to destroy the Post Office had destroyed every building between it and the river. All around were buildings levelled, or falling—but the General Post Office stood erect. It was symbolical of the Spirit of Ireland. Though all around lies death and destruction, though wasted by fire and sword, that very thing which England had put forth her might to crush, stands erect and provides a rallying place for those who follow after. English guns will never destroy the Spirit of Ireland, or the demand for Irish freedom.

We were not stopped by any of the soldiers as we went through the city. It was not until we reached Portobello Bridge that we were told to go back. We had quite a discussion with the soldiers. They said they were under orders not to allow man or woman, boy or girl, to pass without permission from their officer.

"Where is your officer to be found?" I asked.

"He is over there at the public house," said the soldier.

We went over to the public house and found the officer. He was watching his men who were taking supplies from the storehouse. They were probably commandeering. As Kathleen spoke with a strong Dublin accent we made her our spokeswoman. She told the officer that our mother lived in Dundrum, and that we had not been able to get to her since Easter Monday, and that she was sure her mother would be crazy thinking that something had happened to us.

The officer looked at us for a few seconds without saying anything, then said, "I'm sure

THE UNBROKEN TRADITION 171

she would; such a fine lot of girls. Well, you can go through."

"Where's the pass?" asked Kathleen.

"You won't need one," he said. "Just tell the sentry to look over my way."

We went back to the bridge again. This time when we were stopped Kathleen told the soldier to look over at his officer. The soldier looked over, the officer nodded to him, and we passed through.

While we were far out on the Rathmines Road I saw a poster of the Daily Sketch, an English illustrated daily. The poster had a photo of my father on it with the inscription, "James Connolly—The dead rebel leader."

"Thank God!" I cried. "That my mother is so far out of the city. She'll not see that."

We arrived at Dundrum late in the afternoon. We had stopped on our way at shops to buy some provisions for my mother in case she were in need of them. When I came to the cottage the half-door was open, and through it came a sound of weeping, and the frightened crying of my youngest sister. I pulled back the bolt of the half-door and stepped into the cottage. My mother was sitting on a chair weeping. I saw that somehow she had received a copy of the Daily Sketch bearing the false news of my father's death. But she did not know it was false and was mourning my father. When I entered she looked up in amaze, caught her breath, and then run towards me crying,

"My girl, my girl. I thought you were lost to me too."

"You haven't lost any one yet, Mamma," I said. "Papa is wounded and a prisoner, but that is all. They don't shoot or hang prisoners of war. Agna is coming up the path. She'll be here in a minute. Be our own brave little mother again."

Just then Agna came and mother's grief was somewhat alleviated. With her arms around the two of us she said:

"I'd given up all hope of ever seeing you again. Now, I have you and know that your father is not dead. But they'll not let him live long," she cried. "They fear him. They know they can neither bribe nor humble him. He'll always fight them. I've lost Rory too. I don't know what happened to him. He went with his father on Monday. That was the last I saw of him."

Rory is my fifteen-year-old brother, the only son.

"Rory's probably in Jail with the rest of the boys," I said. "They were all imprisoned when they surrendered. He'll be all right there. He's in good company.

We talked long into the morning. Hoping against hope, comforting each other, praying for courage, yet always despairing, we spent the night. The night was long though we tried to make ourselves as comfortable as the cramped quarters and our uneasy minds would allow.

I left the cottage early in the morning to go to Dublin to find a place where my mother and the family could stay. We wanted to be near at hand in case there would be a chance to see my father.

XIV

On Wednesday my mother and sisters came in to Dublin. Agna went up to Dublin Castle to try to see my father. She made a number of attempts to see him, received all sorts of advice, was sent chasing from pillar to post; and finally was told that no visitors would be allowed. The only news she was able to get was from a nurse who told her that Papa was very weak from loss of blood; and that he was not improving.

After that all the news we had of my father was through the newspapers. They told us that he was steadily growing weaker and that his recovery was doubtful. Then we had heard of the murder of Sheehy Skeffington. Agna had met Mrs. Skeffington when she was at Dublin Castle, and had been told the awful news of Skeffington's death. It was a dreadful shock. We had known and admired Sheehy Skeffington, and he had been a great friend of Papa's.

Then day by day the news of executions nearly drove us out of our minds. We heard of the executions of Tom Clarke, and of Padraic Pearse, and of Thomas MacDonagh. Every time we heard the newsboys call out, "Two more executions," or "One more execution" we dreaded to look in the paper for fear we might read my father's name. And yet we must buy the papers.

Every day we heard of further arrests. Every day we saw men being marched off between rows of soldiers. And Mamma had had the added fear of my being arrested given to her. Some one had come to the house and told her that the police were searching for me. I felt that it was not so but could not convince Mamma. At times the awful terror that we were all going to be taken from her took possession of her, and she could not be comforted. We had found out that Rory was imprisoned in Richmond Barracks. Mamma feared and dreaded that he might be shot because of his relationship to his father.

"Willie Pearse was executed because he was Padraic Pearse's brother," she would say when we remonstrated with her. "He was not a leader; he was only a soldier. Rory was a soldier too. How can I be sure that he won't be shot?"

On Sunday afternoon we found a note in the letter box addressed to Mrs. Connolly. Mamma opened it and read: "If Mrs. Connolly will call at Dublin Castle Hospital on Monday or Tuesday after eleven o'clock she can see her husband." Mamma was in terror that Papa's time had come. Every one had been telling her that the fact of Papa's being wounded was a good thing for him; that as long as he was wounded he would not be executed; and that by the time he was well public feeling would have grown so strong the authorities would hesitate to shoot him. "They'll never execute a wounded man" was the cry.

I quieted Mamma's terror somewhat by pointing out that the note said Monday or Tuesday, so the day of his execution could not be either of those days. Still she was in an agony of impatience for Monday morning.

"I'll have to tell him that Rory is in Richmond Barracks," she said.

She had just said this when a knock came to the door. When we opened it Rory and a chum of his stepped inside of the door. They were filthy dirty and their eyes were red rimmed. Sleep clogged their eyes and made speech difficult to them.

"Rory," cried my mother. "And Eamonn—where were you?"

"We were both in Richmond Barracks," said Rory. "We're hungry," he added.

While we got them something to eat they had a wash and came to the table more like themselves.

"We haven't had a real sleep since Easter," said Rory as an excuse for his prodigious yawns.

"Couldn't you sleep in Richmond Barracks?" asked my sister Moira.

"Sleep," he cried. "The room we were in had marked on the door "Accommodation for eleven men" and they put eighty-three of us into it. There was hardly room to stand. We couldn't sit down, we couldn't lie down, we couldn't wash, we couldn't do anything there," he broke off.

We asked him if he knew many of the men in the room with him.

"Yes," he said. "Tom Clarke was in the room with me, and Sean MacDermott, and Major MacBride. But they were removed later."

"How did they come to let you out?"

"O, they were releasing all boys under sixteen."

"Did they ask you anything about your father?" asked Mamma.

"O," said Rory, "I didn't give them my right name. I'm down as Robert Carney, of Bangor, Co. Down."

On Monday morning Mamma went to see my father. Before she went I said, "If you get the chance tell him that we are safe."

"O, I'd be afraid to mention your name," she said.

"Well," I said. "Tell him that Gwendolyn Violet has turned out to be a great walker; that she walked to Dublin. That will satisfy him and quiet his mind."

Gwendolyn Violet was a name bestowed on me by my father when once I had tried to ride my high-horse. And he often used it when he did not desire to refer to me by name.

Before Mamma was allowed to see Papa she was subjected to a most rigorous search. She was also required to give her word that she would not tell him of anything that had gone on outside since the rebellion. Also to promise that she would not bring in anything for him to take his life with. My youngest sister, who was not quite eight years old, and whom Mamma had brought with her was also searched. Mamma came home in a more contented frame of mind. She was sure that he would be spared to her for some time.

On Tuesday I went with Mamma to see my father. There were soldiers on guard at the top of the stairs and in the small alcove leading to Papa's room. They were fully armed and as they stood guard they had their bayonets fixed. All that armed force for a wounded man who could not raise his shoulders from the bed!

In Papa's room there was an officer of the R. A. M. C. all the time with him. Papa had been wounded in the leg, both bones had been fractured. When I saw him his wounded leg was resting in a cage. He was very weak and pale and his voice was very low. I asked him was he suffering much pain.

"No," he said. "But I have been court-martialed to-day. They propped me up in bed. The strain was very great."

I was very much depressed. I had been thinking that there would be no attempt to shoot him till he was well. But then—I knew, that if they courtmartialed him while he was unable to sit up in his bed, they would not hesitate to shoot while he was wounded. I asked him how he got wounded.

"It was while I had gone out to place some men at a certain point. On my way back I was shot above the ankle by a sniper. Both bones in my leg are shattered. I was too far away from the men whom I had just placed to see me, and I was too far from the Post Office to be seen. So I had to crawl back till I was seen. The loss of blood was great. They couldn't get it staunched."

He was very cheerful as he lay in his bed making plans for our future. I know now that he knew what his fate was to be. But he never gave us word or sign that his sentence had been pronounced an hour before we were admitted to him. He gave my mother a message to Sheehy Skeffington asking him to get some of his (Papa's) songs published and to give the proceeds to my mother. It nearly broke my mother's heart to think that she could not tell him that his good friend and comrade had already been murdered by the British. I tried to tell him some things. I told him that the papers had it that Captain Mellowes was still out with his men in the Galway hills. I told him that Laurence Ginnell was fighting for the men in the House of Commons.

"Good man, Larry," he said. "He can always be depended upon."

He was very proud of his men.

"It was a good, clean fight," he said. "The cause cannot die now. The fight will put an end to recruiting. Irishmen now realize the absurdity of fighting for the freedom of another country while their own is still enslaved."

He praised the brave women and girls who had helped in the fight.

"No one can ever say enough to honor or praise them," he said. I mentioned the number of young boys who had been in the fight.

"Rory, you know, was only released on Sunday last along with the other boys of sixteen or under."

"So Rory was in prison," said my father. "How long?"

"Eight days," I answered.

"He fought for his country, and has been imprisoned for his country, and he's not sixteen. He has had a great start in life. Hasn't he, Nora?" he said.

"Tell me," he said. "What happened when you arrived in the North?"

"The men were all dispersed and could not be brought together again," I answered. "When I saw that there would be no fighting there, I tried to come back here. I came by road," I added.

"Did you walk the whole way?" he asked.

"Only from Dundalk," I said. "And when I arrived the fighting was over. I had no chance—I did nothing."

"Nothing," said my father as he reached up his arms and drew me down to his breast. "I think my little woman did as much as any of us."

"There was one young boy, Lillie," he said, turning to my mother, "who was carrying the top of my stretcher when we were leaving the burning Post Office. The street was being swept continually with bullets from machine guns. This young lad was at the head of the stretcher, and if a bullet came near me, he would move his body in such a way that he might receive the bullet instead of me. He was so young looking, although big, that I asked him his age. 'I'm just fourteen, sir,' he answered."

My father's eyes lit up as he was telling the

EAMONN CEANNT

guard at the top of the stair with rifles and fixed bayonets. And in the alcove leading to the room were three more also with fixed bayonets. There was an officer on guard in the room.

When we entered the room Papa had his head turned to the door watching for our coming. When he saw Mamma he said:

"Well, Lillie, I suppose you know what this means?"

"O James! It's not that—it's not that?" my mother wailed.

"Yes, Lillie," he said. "I fell asleep for the first time to-night and they wakened me at eleven and told me that I was to die at dawn."

My mother broke down, laid her head on his bed and sobbed heartbreakingly.

My father patted her head and said, "Don't cry, Lillie, you'll unman me."

"But your beautiful life, James," my mother sobbed. "Your beautiful life."

"Well, Lillie," he said. "Hasn't it been a full life, and isn't this a good end?" My mother still wept.

I was crying too. He turned to me at the other side of the bed and said:

"Don't cry, Nora, there is nothing to cry about."

I said, "I won't cry." He patted my hand and said, "That's my brave girl." He then whispered to me, "Put your hand here," making a movement under the clothes. I put my hand where he indicated. "Put it under the clothes," he said. I did so and he slipped something stiff into my hand.

"Smuggle that out," he said. "It is my last statement."

Mother was sitting at the other side of the bed holding Papa's hand, her face growing grayer and older every minute.

"Remember, Lillie," said my father. "I want you and the girls to go to America. It will be the best place for the girls to get on. Leave the boy at home in Ireland. He was a little brick and I am proud of him."

My mother could only nod her head. Papa tried to cheer her up by telling her about a man who came to the Post Office, during the revolution, to buy a penny stamp; and how indignant he was when he was told he could not get one. "Don't know what Dublin is coming to when you can't buy a stamp at the Post Office," he said.

Papa then turned to me and said, "I heard that poor Skeffington was killed." I said, "Yes." And then I told him that all his staff, that all the best men in Ireland were gone. He was silent for a while, then said, "I am glad I am going with them." I think he thought he was the first to be executed. I told him that the papers that day had said, that it was promised in the House of Commons that there would be no more shootings. "England's promises," was all he said to that.

The officer then told us that we had only five minutes more. My mother was nearly overcome; we had to give her water. Papa tried to clasp her in his arms but he could only lift his head and shoulders from the bed. The officer said, "Time is up." Papa turned to say "Good-by" to me. I could not speak. "Go to mother," he said.

I tried to bring her away. I could not move her. She stood as if turned to stone. A nurse came forward and helped her away. I ran back and kissed my father again. "Nora, I'm proud of you," said my father. I kissed him again, then the door was shut and we saw him no more.

We were brought back to the house. Mother

went to the window, pulled back the curtain, and stood watching for the dawn, moaning all the while. I thought her heart would break and that she would die too.

When dawn was past and we knew that my father was dead, I opened the stiff piece of paper he had given me, and read to my mother, my brother and sisters the Last Statement of my father.

This is what I read:

To the Field General Court Martial, held at Dublin Castle, on May 9, 1916.

The evidence mainly went to establish the fact that the accused, James Connolly, was in command at the General Post Office, and was also the Commandant-General of the Dublin Division. Two of the witnesses, however, strove to bring in alleged instances of wantonly risking the lives of prisoners. The Court held that these charges were *irrelevant* and could not be placed against the prisoner.

I do not wish to make any defense except against charges of wanton cruelty to prisoners. These trifling allegations, that have been made, if they record facts that really happened, deal only with the almost unavoidable incidents of a hurried uprising against long established authority, and nowhere show evidence of set purpose to wantonly injure unarmed persons.

We went out to break the connection between this country and the British Empire, and to establish an Irish Republic. We believed that the call we then issued to the people of Ireland, was a nobler call, in a holier cause, than any call issued to them during this war, having any connection with the war. We succeeded in proving that Irishmen are ready to die endeavoring to win for Ireland those national rights, which the British Government has been asking them to die to win for Belgium. As long as that remains the case the cause of Irish Freedom is safe.

Believing that the British Government has no right in Ireland, never had any right in Ireland, and never can have any right in Ireland, the presence, in any one generation of Irishmen, of even a respectable minority, ready to die to affirm that truth, makes that government forever a usurpation and a crime against human progress.

I personally thank God that I have lived to see the day when thousands of Irishmen and boys, and hundreds of Irish women and girls were ready to affirm that truth, and to attest it with their lives if need be.

(Signed) JAMES CONNOLLY, Commandant-General,
Dublin Division, Army of the Irish Republic.

XV

WE went to Dublin Castle that morning to ask for his body. It was refused to us. The authorities were not permitting even a coffin, we were told. But a kind nurse had cut off a lock of Papa's hair and this she gave to Mamma.

That was all there was left of him for us.

We saw Father Aloyisus who had attended my father to Kilmainham jail where he had been shot.

"How did they shoot him—how could they shoot him? He couldn't sit up in his bed. He couldn't stand up to be shot," I cried. "How was he shot?"

"It was a terrible shock to me," said Father Aloyisus. "I had been with him that evening and I promised to come to him this afternoon. I felt sure there would be no more executions —at least that is how I read the words of Mr. Asquith. And your father was so much easier than he had been. I was sure that he would get his first night's real rest."

"But, how did they shoot him, Father?"

"The ambulance that brought you home from him came for me. I was astonished. I had felt so sure that I would not be needed that for the first time since the rising I locked the doors. And some time after two, I was knocked up. The ambulance brought me to your father. He was a wonderful man. I am sorry to say that of all men who have been executed, he was the only one I did not know personally. Though I knew of him and admired his work. I will always thank God as long as I live that He permitted me to be with your father till he was dead. Such a wonderful man he was. Such concentration of mind."

"Yes, Father, but they shot him—how?"

"They carried him from his bed in an ambulance stretcher down to a waiting ambulance and drove him to Kilmainham Jail. They carried him from the ambulance to the Jail yard and put him on a chair. . . . He was very brave and cool. . . . I said to him, 'Will you pray for the men who are about to shoot you,' and he said, 'I will say a prayer for all brave men who do their duty.' . . . His prayer was, 'Forgive them for they know not what they do.' . . . And then they shot him. . . ."

"What did they do with him, then?" whispered my mother.

"They took the body to Arbor Hill Barracks. All the men who were executed are there."

Papa had told mother to ask for his personal effects. And mother had asked for them. We only received some of his underclothes and the night clothes he wore in bed while he was wounded. Papa had said that the authorities had his watch, his pocketbook, and his uniform. But the officer in charge knew nothing about them.

Mother made many inquiries. But it was not until she went in person to General Maxwell that she succeeded in having the pocket book returned to her. Major Price, Chief Intelligence Officer in Ireland, had told her that they were keeping it for evidence.

Evidence—what more evidence did they require against a man they had executed?

Some time afterwards we recovered his watch; but we never found his uniform. And since I came to America I have been shown that a copy of the paper my father edited with his last corrections upon it, was put upon the market by a careful British officer who had figured out its value as a souvenir.

And then the whispered warnings came again to awaken my mother's fear. Some messages reached her that the police were again looking for me. Nor could I convince her otherwise. She begged and pleaded with me to go away from Dublin so that I would not be arrested. So that she might feel more at ease in her mind, I went to Belfast.

Even then she did not feel that I was safe. She came to Belfast and asked me to try to get to America alone. In accordance with my father's last wish she had applied for passports to take us all to America, or to take the girls. But the British authorities felt that the arrival of Mrs. Connolly and her five daughters in America would be prejudicial to the interests of the Realm; and refused her the passports. She had gone again and again to the authorities, only to be sent hither and thither on a fool's errand. And as she despaired of ever getting them she asked me to make any attempt I could and to use whatever means I could to get to America.

"Let them see that your comings and goings are not dependent on their goodwill."

And I to please her left Ireland and crossed to England. There I applied for a passport; and was given one. Not as the daughter of James Connolly, however.

It was the last week of June that we received the final refusal of our request for passports, and on the third week of July I sailed from Liverpool. I arrived in New York the first day of August, nineteen hundred and sixteen.

XVI

For the benefit of the reader in whose mind there might rise some confusion with regard to the demobilization of the Irish Volunteers, and how this demobilization order could spoil the plans for the Rising, and why Eoin Mac-Neill had the power to send out such an order. I am adding the following statement:

When the Irish Volunteers were first organized, it was necessary to have a man known throughout Ireland, a man of some reputation and authority, as the head of the organization. Eoin MacNeill was such a man. He was an authority on Irish History and Ancient Ireland. Also, what was more necessary, he was an unknown quantity to the English Government. Had there been elected as President a man well known as a revolutionary and as an Extremist, there would have been short work made of the Irish Volunteers. The English Government would then have known immediately that the Irish Volunteers were being organized, drilled, and supplied with arms for the sole purpose of a rebellion against it, and would have given it no opportunity to spread and grow, and become disciplined. As it was, with MacNeill as the President, whom they knew as a rather conservative, academic person, whose politics at that time were more of the Home Rule order than anything else, they felt quite at ease and contented about the growth of the Irish Volunteers.

MacNeill, although friendly with, and because of the Irish Volunteers in continual contact with, the revolutionary members, was not a member of the Revolutionary Organization. He was not of the type to which revolutionists belong. His mind was of the academic order which must weigh all things, consider well all actions, and count the cost. A true revolutionist must never count the cost, for he knows that a revolution always repays itself, though it cost blood, and through it life be lost and sacrifice made. He knows that the flame of the ideal which caused the revolution burns all the more brightly, and steadily, and thus attracts more men and minds, and because of the life-blood and sacrifice becomes more enduring.

That a man of MacNeill's type of mind

196 THE UNBROKEN TRADITION

should have gone so far along the road to revolution is the extraordinary thing. Due credit should be given to him for that, although he did fail his comrades at the critical moment.

MacNeill was made President, and all orders affecting the organization as a whole, that is all important orders, came from him under his signature. Therefore, when an order came with his signature, the Irish Volunteers obeyed it unquestioningly.

Padraic Pearse as Commandant-General of the Irish Volunteers was Chief in military affairs. And that is where the Irish Volunteers made the first mistake. The office of President should have been of a purely civil character. So that when a military order was issued from Headquarters, it would bear, not the signature of the President but the signature of the Military chief. That this would have been difficult, I am aware,—it is so easy to see mistakes after they are made.

MacNeill, through the columns of the *Irish Volunteer* (the official organ of the Irish Volunteers), always preached prudence, and a waiting policy. He advised the Volunteers not to be the first to attack, but to wait to be attacked. He counseled them to recruit their ranks, so that when the war was ended their number would reach three hundred thousand; and that an armed force of three hundred thousand men would then be in a position to demand the freedom of Ireland from England. Still, as before, this counsel was regarded by the rank and file of the Irish Volunteers as a necessary evil, knowing that it is not wise policy to show your hand to the enemy before the appointed time.

The revolutionary members, all this time, were completing their plans, strengthening the organization, and waiting eagerly and hopefully for the days to pass, and the Day of all days to come. Every time they thought of the approaching day they were quietly exultant. They knew that their chance of success was greater than it had ever been since the days of Shane and Hugh O'Neill. And they joyfully, and prayerfully thanked God that the opportunity had come in their day. All things went well, their plans matured, and at last they were ready for the fight.

The order for mobilizing was sent through the length and breadth of Ireland, and it was signed by Eoin MacNeill. The order was received and obeyed by the Irish Volunteers.

Then, on Good Friday, came the news that Roger Casement was arrested.

Roger Casement had gone to Germany, shortly after the outbreak of the war, to seek an expression of goodwill toward Ireland from Germany. Germany knew that Ireland was held in subjection to England, contrary to the wishes of the vast majority of the Irish people, and that Ireland had always considered the enemy of her oppressor as her friend. Germany knew that when Spain was England's enemy, Ireland had sought the assistance of the Spanish King, and when France was the enemy of England, Wolfe Tone and Robert Emmet had both sought the aid of France; she knew that when England was at war with the Boers, Irishmen had organized a brigade, and gone to South Africa, in the hope of helping to defeat the English enemy. She knew, that then, as now, Ireland was anti-British, and would remain so. Therefore, Germany declared her goodwill towards Ireland, and to the present day Ireland has been free from the terrors of Zeppelin raids, and there has been no German bombardment of our coast.

Soon after arriving in Germany, Roger Casement lost touch with Irish affairs. He still believed that the Irish Volunteers were as badly armed as when he left Ireland. He did not know of the plans for the rising, nor did he know who were to be the leaders, or whether they had military ability or not.

He did not know that the leaders, acting on the expression of goodwill, had asked Germany to send them some arms. I wish to make it plain that Germany never made an offer to the men in Ireland, that she gave nothing to them, not even the expression of goodwill, till she was asked, and that when a request for aid came from Ireland, it was not for money (England has kept us so poor that we have almost learned to do without money), nor was it for men, but for arms, guns, and ammunition. All that Germany promised in return to the request, was that she would make the attempt to send us a certain amount of arms, but as the ship would have to run the gauntlet of the British fleet, she would promise nothing.

This answer was satisfactory to the revolutionary leaders. A date was set for the ship to arrive, and a place designated.

After setting the date and sending it on to Germany, the leaders found that it was necessary to change the date. Word was sent to

Germany, but only arrived there after the shipload of arms had set out.

About this time Roger Casement heard that a revolution was about to take place. He asked that he be sent over to Ireland. There was some demur at this, but finally they consented and gave him a submarine. With him on the submarine went two followers of Casement.

The shipload of arms arrived on the first appointed date but the men in Ireland, not knowing that their final message had been too late, had no one there to meet it. Consequently, the ship had to hang about for a number of hours, and finally attracted the suspicion of the fleet which was in Queenstown Harbor. When challenged by the fleet, knowing that subterfuge was hopeless, the Captain ran up the German flag, and sunk the vessel with all the arms and ammunition.

Shortly after this, the submarine with Casement and the two other men arrived off the Irish coast. They were landed with the aid of a collapsible boat belonging to the submarine. Casement, after sending a message to MacNeill advising against the Rising, and saying in the message that Germany had failed

THE UNBROKEN TRADITION 201

us, sought shelter in an old ruin. One of the men managed to make his way into the country and so escaped. Casement was arrested.

Before he was hanged he said that his whole object in coming to Ireland was to prevent the Revolution. He did not do so, but was, perhaps, the primary cause of its failure.

Acting on Casement's message and believing it, MacNeill sent out the demobilizing orders. He had sent out many of them before the other leaders became aware of it. He also gave instructions to the Secretary of the Irish Volunteers to send out more. Then Pearse and MacDonagh had a conference with him. After the conference he said to the Secretary that although the thing was hopeless, he was afraid it must go on.

He knew that the revolutionary leaders had decided that the revolution must take place, even though the loss of the arms had seriously crippled their plans. He knew that a disarmament of the Irish Volunteers had been threatened, also the imprisonment of the leaders. He knew that the Volunteers would resist the disarming, and that the leaders still thought that they would have a good fighting chance.

When he knew that the fight would go on in

202 THE UNBROKEN TRADITION

Dublin, in spite of his order, he began to weigh up the consequences, and saw nothing before the Irish Volunteers save death and imprisonment. The responsibility of allowing these men to go out to meet these, weighed too heavily on him, and he thought that he might save the Irish Volunteers in the country from them. He then had a message inserted in the Sunday *Independent,* a paper that went to all the nooks and corners of the country, to the effect that:

"All Volunteer maneuvers for Sunday are canceled. Volunteers everywhere will obey this order.
(Signed) Eoin MacNeill.

It was not until Sunday morning that the other leaders knew of this demobilization order in the paper.

The consequences of this order in the paper, and the orders that were sent out before it, I have already told.